WITH THE WORD

A BIBLE STUDY AND DEVOTIONAL GUIDE
FOR GROUPS OR INDIVIDUALS

Faith & Life Resources

Harrisonburg, VA and Waterloo, ON

With the Word: Psalms
Copyright © 2011 by Faith & Life Resources, Harrisonburg, Virginia 22802
     Released simultaneously in Canada by Faith & Life Resources,
     Waterloo, Ontario N2L 6H7. All rights reserved.
International Standard Book Number: 978-0-8361-9570-5
Printed in United States of America
Cover and interior design by Merrill R. Miller

Sessions from *Adult Bible Study Teacher* and *Adult Bible Study Student*, along with
Rejoice! daily devotions were all used in the writing of *With the Word: Psalms*.

To order or request information, please call 1-800-245-7894 in the U.S. or
1-800-631-6535 in Canada. Or visit www.faithandliferesources.org.

15 14 13 12 11   10 9 8 7 6 5 4 3 2 1

Faith & Life Resources

Table of contents

INTRODUCTION
5

SESSION FORMAT
7

1. THE RIGHT WAY (PSALM 1)
8

2. CARING FOR GOD'S CREATION (PSALM 8)
14

3. GOD'S GLORY IN CREATION AND THE LAW (PSALM 19)
20

4. GOD'S COMFORT AND REASSURANCE (PSALM 23)
26

5. JOY IN FORGIVENESS (PSALM 32)
32

6. TELL THE STORY (PSALM 78)
38

7. LET PRAISE CONTINUE (PSALM 104)
44

8. DON'T BE AFRAID (PSALM 121)
50

9. SEARCHED AND KNOWN BY GOD (PSALM 139)
56

10. WORTHY OF PRAISE (PSALM 145)
62

Introduction

Welcome to *With the Word*! This exciting new series from Faith & Life Resources invites you to draw closer to God by spending time with the Word through Bible study and daily devotions.

Studying the Psalms

The influence of the book of Psalms on Jewish and Christian traditions, both in terms of the worship of the community and the spiritual experience of countless individuals, is immense. Of all the Old Testament books, Psalms has a special place in the hearts and minds of Christians—with every believer having a favorite psalm or two.

This grand collection of psalms is a treasured *hymnbook*, inviting and expressing the people's praise to their sovereign God. Here is also a *prayer book*, voicing the needs of individuals and the community in times of trouble. Finally, the book of Psalms serves as an *instruction book*, as indicated in the opening psalm's invitation to "meditate day and night" on the life-giving word of God's instruction for living (1:2; cf. Psalm 19; 119).

The book of Psalms is a treasury of experiences accumulated by generations of people who nourished their hopes and anxieties as they clung to their values and their faith in God. The Psalms belong to a Bible category known as the Wisdom books because they are designed to teach something about how to live.

Readers of these sacred poems soon discover that each psalm speaks for itself. While commentaries may provide some helpful background, alert readers to linkage with words and themes, and stimulate the imagination for application, it will not replace repeated readings of a psalm in order to hear God speak through the psalm's own distinctive structure and world of words.

Only through reading the psalms, slowly and reflectively, will we find ourselves in these ancient Hebrew Scriptures, which draw us into the presence of the sovereign God.

As these texts become our prayers and heart songs, we will come to know ourselves more fully and to know God more surely.

—from James H. Waltner, *Psalms*, Believers Church Bible Commentary (Scottdale, Pa.: Herald Press, 2006), 17–19. Used by permission.

Session format

* *

In this volume on Psalms, you will find ten sessions for either group or individual use. The easy-to-use format starts with an in-depth Bible study and ends with seven short devotionals designed to be read in the days after the session. Here's a guide to each session:

- **Opening:** The opening of the Bible study portion calls you to into the session through a summary of the text and a few questions for reflection. Before you begin each session, take time to read the text reflectively.

- **For the leader:** These are ideas for how to use the material in a group setting. If using the material individually, omit this section.

- **Understanding God's Word:** This section makes connections made between the session's text and today's world.

- **Connecting with God's Word:** This is the heart of the guide; it's the in-depth Bible study that calls you to examine specific parts of the session's text. The writer gives background for a few verses of text, then outlines a series of questions for personal reflection or discussion. These questions always invite you to make connections between the biblical text and your own life.

- **Closing:** The Bible study portion of the session then closes with a brief time of worship and wrapping up.

- **Devotionals:** Immediately after the sessions you will find seven short devotionals on the session's text. Each devotional starts with a Scripture verse, includes a meditation, and ends with a prayer. Use these seven inspiring devotionals in the days after the session as way to keep the text in your heart and mind.

Spend time *With the Word* today!

The right way

PSALM 1

* *

Opening

Psalm 1 states that fulfillment in life for the righteous does not come from following the counsel, lifestyle, and influence of the wicked. Rather, their godly quality of life derives from a singular investment, trust, and obedience to the law that God has given to them.

Review newspaper or magazine accounts of people who have done well and are greatly respected in their community as well as stories of those who have failed and are in disfavor in their neighborhood. Share times when you lived up to your community ideals. Discuss the times you failed to perform in a manner that benefited your neighborhood?

Understanding God's Word

An elderly woman increased her television viewing after she retired. Because she could no longer get out much, she tuned in to her favorite crime shows and to local news programs that tended to highlight crime. The more she watched, the more frightened she became of leaving her home, particularly at night. She warned anyone who would listen about potential dangers in the street. While crime decreased around her, her fears increased.

Television is a welcome companion for many people. But they must

* *

For the leader

Bring copies of local newspapers and magazines.

1. Pray for one another about times when attendees have caused harm in their neighborly relations. Thank God for those events in which attendees have been faithful in their life-witness to the community.

2. Read Psalm 1 in unison. Or ask half of the class to read verses 1-3 and the other half to read verses 4-6.

be careful about what they watch. Messages from television influence our thinking. Psalm 1 emphasizes that we should fill our time and our minds with things that are wholesome and helpful. Reading and studying the Torah (God's teachings), it says, leads to happiness and a productive life.

Connecting with God's Word

The Psalms belong to a Bible category known as the Wisdom books, because they are designed to teach something about how to live. A typical technique of Wisdom sayings is to set up a contrast. In the case of Psalm 1, the contrast is between the righteous and the wicked. The purpose of the psalm is to encourage people to follow the Torah (Hebrew for "instruction") that God has given so we can lead a happy and successful life. It may have been composed as an opening to the book of Psalms.

To be happy, avoid the following things (1:1)

The first verse of this psalm—and the opener for the entire book of psalms—begins with the Hebrew word *ashre*, translated "happy" (*NRSV*) or "blessed" (*NIV*). *Ashre* begins with the first letter of the Hebrew alphabet, *aleph*.

Verse 1 also begins a series of negative statements, all of which begin with *bet*, the second letter of the Hebrew alphabet. The psalmist tells the reader which behaviors are to be avoided in three crisp verbal statements: Do not walk . . . Do not stand . . . Do not sit. . . .

The righteous person should avoid the counsel of the wicked, the way of sinners, and the seat of scoffers. Notice that it is not the wicked, the sinners, and the scoffers who are to be avoided. Rather, it is their behavior, their thinking, and their approach to life and other people.

- Why does Psalm 1 begin with behaviors to be avoided? Do negative statements prepare us to consider the alternate positive options? Do you prefer to hear the "don'ts" before the "do's"?

- What is important about the fact that the first word of Psalm 1:1 begins with the first letter of the Hebrew alphabet? What do you think the psalmist intended with this choice?

- How easy is it for you to separate the behavior and thinking from the person who is expressing or living unacceptable beliefs or lifestyles?

To be happy, do the following things (1:2-3)

The second verse describes the righteous person positively, as one who delights in the instruction of Yahweh (the Hebrew name translated as "the Lord") and meditates on it day and night.

Instruction is a better translation of the Hebrew word *torah* than *law*. When we think of law, we think of crime and punishment. God's *torah* is not always accompanied by punishments (see Exodus 20:12-17), because that is not its main concern. The Lord gives instruction to show humans how to live, not to punish them for disobeying laws.

- Why is our first response to *law* often negative? Why do we often come to view laws as good and wholesome for the family and community?

- Does it help you to understand that the proper meaning of *torah* "law" is "instruction"? What difference does this make in your living?

- Does it reassure you that the Lord's first desire is to show us how to live life? If so, how?

The short lifespan of wickedness (1:4-6)

The fourth verse returns to the first by picking up the reference to the wicked. The wicked, unlike firmly planted righteous people, are like chaff that is blown away by the wind. Wickedness is seen to be impermanent. It is not deeply rooted, as is righteousness.

According to Psalm 1, the wicked will not stand in the judgment. They will not be able to hold their position. The Jewish Publication Society translation reads, "The wicked will not survive judgment."

The second group in verse 1, the sinners, is then addressed. They will not stand in the congregation of the righteous. The righteous (or "just") are not perfect human beings. They are those who do what is right, what is just, in the context of the community. The Lord knows the way of the righteous because this is the Lord's own way.

- The psalmist describes the wicked as chaff. Chaff is understood by farmers and others in the agricultural segment of our economy. Restate this image so that it would be understandable in urban households.

- What resources and sources of strength have enabled the faithful to stand as righteous members of God's family?

- What evidences do you see that support the reality that wickedness has a short lifespan?

Closing

1. Name one way you will impress on yourself and another to make Psalm 1 an essential part of your life and thought this week.

2. Close by reading Psalm 1 in unison.

* * * * * * * * * * * * * * * * *

Devotional 1

Happy are those who do not follow the advice of the wicked, or take the path that sinners tread. —Psalm 1:1

Joris Wippe (d. 1558), whose story is recorded in the *Martyrs Mirror*, fits the person described in Psalm 1. As a dyer, Wippe worked with cloth dealers. He was highly respected by his neighbors in Dordrecht, the Netherlands.

When Joris was arrested for being an Anabaptist, the tradespeople believed that the officials would show him leniency. The leaders didn't want to execute him for heresy. The city executioner refused to kill him. To avoid public outrage, Wippe was drowned in a barrel in his cell rather than executed in front of the people.

While waiting for his execution, Wippe was comforted by the Psalms. He wrote to his family, "I charge you, Joos and Hansken, that . . . you will care for your three little sisters, and for Pierken, and teach them to read and to work, so that they may grow up in all righteousness, to the honor of God and the salvation of their souls." *—Bob Hoffman*

May we walk righteously and obediently with God today, wherever the path may lead.

* * * * * * * * * * * * * * *

Devotional 2

Their delight is in the law of the Lord, and on his law they meditate day and night. —Psalm 1:2

Frank Laubach encouraged people to play "the game of minutes." He wanted all to turn their attention to God every minute of the day. He called believers to listen to the Holy Spirit just as the psalmist challenged the people to meditate on the law. Christians do not meditate on the law given to Moses as much as we open ourselves to live out the life of Christ as the Holy Spirit empowers us.

The apostle Paul said that the "the law was our disciplinarian until Christ came, so that we might be justified by faith" (Galatians 3:24). The law is good and it guides us to know right behavior. But it is the Spirit that enables us to be changed in our basic being, as God in Christ gives us new life. While it is good to meditate on the law, it is better to commune with Christ and be empowered beyond the usual demands of life. *—William Keeney*

Jesus, help me to live close enough to you to be ready at all times to hear your Holy Spirit speak. Empower me to follow obediently and with joy.

* * * * * * * * * * * * * *

Devotional 3

Their delight is in the law of the LORD, and on his law they meditate day and night. —Psalm 1:2

The psalmist asks us to meditate day and night on God's law—the wise words that make up the Scriptures. This is a tall order in our noisy world where we are constantly bombarded with other words.

Ignatius of Loyola encourages us to use our senses in the discipline of meditation. Listen for God's voice in birdsong, music, and the serenity of silence. Savor the various flavors and textures of your food today, and thank the Creator. Breathing deeply reminds us of God's "breath of life" sustaining us. Look at greenery and recall the flourishing tree in Psalm 1:3 and Jeremiah 17:8.

To meditate may mean using our waiting time to listen to God's words. Or memorizing the daily devotional responses and repeating them throughout the day. Or using a favorite Psalm as a bedtime prayer. However we do it, weaving God's thoughts into the fabric of our daily lives can bring delight in our relationship with God. *–Annie Lind*

Let the words of my mouth and the meditation of my heart be acceptable to you, O LORD, my rock and my redeemer (Psalm 19:14).

* * * * * * * * * * * * * * * *

Devotional 4

Their delight is in the law of the Lord, and on his law they meditate day and night.
—Psalm 1:2

Psalm 1 is a favorite psalm from my childhood. I liked its rhythm and contrasts. The difference between a living, stable, fruitful tree and dead, useless chaff is a powerful picture of the contrast between the righteous and the wicked.

The righteous one is happy, taking delight in meditating on the Lord's law. That delight extends to all of life and its opportunities to share the fruit of knowing God and the Word. It includes thankfulness for life and for the Lord's watchful care.

I need to understand and experience more of the life and fruitfulness of the tree. Firm roots draw up life-giving water continually, not only in a fifteen-minute devotional time.

In *The Living Reminder*, Henri Nouwen wrote, "A prayerful life is not a life in which we say many prayers, but a life in which nothing, absolutely nothing, is done, said, or understood independently of him who is the origin and purpose of our existence."
–Janet Gehman

Thank you, Lord, for the delight that comes from meditating on your Word and living an obedient, fruitful life every day.

* * * * * * * * * * * * * * * *

Devotional 5

Their delight is in the law of the LORD, and on his law they meditate day and night.
—Psalm 1:2

Today people are bombarded daily by the "advice of the wicked" through television, magazines, books, and movies. As we listen to voices of selfish ambition and violence, the greater our chances of moving away from God.

How can we guard against this downward spiral? Psalm 1 encourages us to delight in the law of the Lord, to begin each day with the Word of God, and to mediate on it constantly. We can soak it up like tree roots soak up life-giving water.

How does a busy person meditate "day and night"? I put verses on cards and paste them above the sink. I rehearse them as I walk the dog, wait in a traffic jam, swim laps in a pool, and listen to Scripture songs.

As we are immersed in God's Word, we resemble a deeply rooted and fruitful tree. When adversities come, we stand firm in the faith, bearing fruit to the glory of God. *–Helen Grace Lescheid*

Since I am prone to wander, Lord, I will feed on your Word and choose to walk in your ways.

* * * * * * * * * * * * * * *
Devotional 6

They are like trees planted by streams of water, which yield their fruit in its season.... In all they do, they prosper. —Psalm 1:3

I grew up near a city park with a clear, sparkling stream. Along the banks were several stately trees with massive limbs and soaring branches. These trees were selected for their site by the park's arborists.

The psalmist portrays those who take delight in the law of the Lord as trees planted by streams of water. The picture reminds us of the trees in the garden of Eden: "pleasant to the sight and good for food" (Genesis 2:9) and the trees in the future new Jerusalem that produce fruit each month and whose leaves are "for the healing of the nations" (Revelation 22:2).

God has planted your family, your community, and your church where you live now. You are in a unique place to grow, send down roots, flourish, and be productive. God knows the ideal climate and conditions suited for fruitfulness. Let us recognize that we have been placed in a chosen site where God wants us to set down roots and grow. *—Ray Harris*

Thank God for the people, opportunities, and situations in your life that you see as his grace and provision for you.

* * * * * * * * * * * * * * *
Devotional 7

The Lord watches over the way of the righteous, but the way of the wicked will perish. —Psalm 1:6

If the Lord watches out for the righteous, why do the wicked take so long to perish? Psalm 1 tells us that being good ensures a reward. But is that what we see? Is that what we should teach our children: the good guys always win? How practical is that?

The editor of the Psalms chose this one to head the list. The 149 psalms that follow express not only faith and worship, but also skepticism, anguish, doubt, grief, rage, and frustration with God's delay in creating justice. Yet the psalmist expects us to pass on a vision of the way the world ought to be—the way God expects it to be. The way it will be.

Some may think it is futile to teach peace, mutual aid, accountability, and the stories of our faith heroes following Jesus. But we know better. This psalm assures us that God's will shall be done on earth as it is in heaven. The eyes of faith tell us, God's way prevails. *—Frank Ramirez*

Imagine praying this psalm with faithful people you have known, and praise God for their example.

Caring for God's creation

Psalm 8

* *

Opening

Good parents do not give their children to a person who is incompetent to care for them and then trust that caregiver to raise them to adulthood. In Psalm 8, God lovingly and carefully created the moon, stars, animals, birds, and fish, then turned their care and management over to humans.

God is confident that humans can care for the created world. We can either rise to the challenge or fail miserably. What does it mean that humans have been given "dominion" over creation and that all things have been put "under [our] feet"? What issues in your community call for Christians to be stewards of the earth?

How do you care for that segment of creation under your dominion? Share ways that you can work with others to care for God's creation. Pray that each may fulfill his or her mandate as God's steward.

Understanding God's Word

Malcolm Boyd wrote *Are You Running with Me Jesus?* in the sixties. He believed that the traditional practices of prayer and the set prayers of the

* *

For the leader

Bring published articles and pictures that illustrate ways humans treat God's creation.

Psalm 8 is a hymn praising the Lord. Yahweh (Lord, in capitals) is called upon and then addressed as our Adonai (Lord with lowercase letters). The New Revised Standard Version uses Lord/Lord: "O Lord, our Sovereign." Psalm 8 begins and ends with the same line, using identical words of adoration. This poetic technique of "packaging" is also used in Psalm 103, 104, 149, and 150.

Read Psalm 8 aloud as a litany. Follow these instructions:

- *All* read verse 1a in unison.
- *Women* read verses 1b-2.
- *Men* read verses 3-4.
- *Women* read verses 5-8.
- *All* read verse 9 in unison.

church were no longer as useful as they once were. He felt that in an age of activism, Christians need to be able to talk to God while on the go. His writing was a reminder that God is ever-present and ought to be a part of everything we do. God has come to us as a friend.

In Psalm 8, the writer reflects on the transcendence of God. Transcendence is the reality that goes beyond the created world. As such, we do not easily access transcendence through our regular human channels of communication. When we try to speak of the transcendence of God, words fail us. Our words are inadequate to express the wonder and awe that overtakes us when we meditate on the grace and greatness of God.

Psalm 8, like most psalms, is a prayer spoken to God in formal (the temple and later the synagogue) and informal settings. It begins by addressing God directly. Two different Hebrew words for God appear in the first verse, translated as "O, LORD, our Lord." The first word for God is *Yahweh*, but written in Hebrew as four consonants: YHWH—the God of Israel. The second is *Adonai*. In Jewish practice, *Adonai*, or *Lord*, was substituted for God's name to protect it from misuse. By using both *Yahweh* and *Adonai*, the psalmist establishes that the God of Israel is the majestic God, not just any god.

Connecting with God's Word

Why does God care about us? (8:3-4)
The psalmist looks at human beings from two perspectives. First he imagines what human beings must look like in the eyes of God. Then he notices how humans appear in the eyes of other people. He believes that humans must look insignificant in the eyes of God. It is amazing that God, who made the heavens and the world, is also concerned about humans and cares for them. Humans are fragile. They are also mortal—here for a while and then gone. But God still remembers them.

- Describe a time when you caught a glimpse of the transcendence of God. How did you respond?

- Share about a time when you felt weak but, by God's strength, you were able to overcome the odds.

- In light of God's view of humans, how do we relate to fellow humans with their diverse languages, cultures, and lifestyles?

The special position of human beings (8:5-8)
Next the psalmist thinks about humans from the viewpoint of humans. Humans think highly of themselves. While humans are part of the created

world, they are elevated to a little lower than gods (or God). Humans rule over all other created things. This is an awesome responsibility, but humans have not always managed well.

- The psalmist recognizes that God made us glorious creatures with dignity and worth. Why has God given glory and honor to mere humans?

- What expectations are placed on humans since God values people so highly?

- How does one rule over the works of God's hands, over the other creatures? What are the day-to-day implications?

A majestic name (8:9)

The psalm ends as it began; the first and last verses are exactly the same. This structure is called an *inclusio*. The repetition of the first verse at the end signals the end of the psalm. This was necessary because biblical Hebrew did not provide numbers or titles for the psalms. You knew that you were at the end of a poem when you heard the first lines repeated. Most of the psalms end with a word of praise or an expression of hope.

- What affect does this *inclusio* have as you reflect on the psalm? Does it underscore the uniqueness and majesty of God?

- For each letter of the word *majestic*, list attributes of God that have come to you through this session.

- Names are important. What names for God are meaningful to you? Explain why they are important.

Closing

1. State one way you will exercise your God-given dominion duties this week.

2. Sing a hymn of praise to God for being both majestic and caring for all peoples.

3. Close by reading Psalm 8 in unison.

DEVOTIONALS

* *

Devotional 1

O LORD, our Sovereign, how majestic is your name in all the earth! —Psalm 8:1

In my primary Sunday school class, we used body language to express the majesty of this psalm. Even today, it is hard to recite it without using my hands and arms.

God's creation is mind boggling. We look at the stars with a naked eye and count two thousand of them. By telescope we see a hundred billion stars, yet we still don't know everything about the universe.

Amazingly, all this celestial wonder can be studied through a few simple laws and equations. To Albert Einstein, that was the greatest miracle. He wrote, "The most incomprehensible thing about the universe is that it is comprehensible."

The most incomprehensible thing is that our Creator knows and understands us, and that we, in turn, can know God. Verse 2 affirms that even infants and children can praise God. And Jesus quoted this verse to the indignant priests when he drove the moneychangers from the temple (see Matthew 21:16). *–LaVerna Klippenstein*

"O LORD, our Sovereign, how majestic is your name in all the earth!" What a wonderful privilege to be your child! With all my heart, I thank you!

* * * * * * * * * * * * * * * * * *

Devotional 2

Out of the mouths of babes and infants you have founded a bulwark because of your foes, to silence the enemy and the avenger. —Psalm 8:2

I spoke with a plant manager of a firm that would soon relocate to my community. I asked him how he had come to work for the company. "When I was plant manager in my previous job," he said, "I was told that downsizing was coming and that I was the person to make these layoff decisions. I struggled with this.

"Knowing what I was required to do the next day, my young son asked me at dinner what I did at work that day. I told him I had had a bad day and that I was required to do something the next day that I didn't want to do. My son innocently replied, 'If you really don't want to do it, then don't do it.'"

Those words were all he needed to hear. He resigned and found employment in a smaller business. "I'm a lot happier, thanks to advice from my young son."

Years earlier, the psalmist proclaimed that out of the mouths of children, God teaches us how to be strong and faithful. *–Fred Steiner*

God, when I seek your help, remind me to listen to the voices of children. From them I will learn to be strong.

* * * * * * * * * * * * * * * *

Devotional 3

When I look at your heavens . . . the moon and the stars that you have established; what are human beings that you are mindful of them? —Psalms 8:3-4

During Bible school, as I watched the staff go about its activities, I found myself counting the gifts I was lacking. "I can't sing like Lynette, do crafts like Gloria, or be a good mom like Cori."

Then I felt low. I had wasted five minutes counting my "can't's" regarding things that weren't important to God. Instead of thanking God for the gifts and abilities I enjoyed, I had thought about what I didn't have.

The cure for self-deprecation is praise. When we focus on God, we can't concentrate on our shortcomings. God has big plans for us, no matter how small we feel. When the psalmist asked, "What are human beings that you are mindful of them?" (v. 4), he was feeling inconsequential. But then he said that we are in charge of the creation (v. 6). We can't feel unimportant when given such a great responsibility.

When you feel unimportant, look around. That tree, flower, or bird—God made it for you. God gives us gifts daily to remind us how important we are to him. –Dawn Mast

God of creation, sometimes I am so hard on myself I forget I am your creation. Thank you for loving me and trusting me to take care of your world.

* * * * * * * * * * * * * * *

Devotional 4

What are human beings that you are mindful of them, mortals that you care for them? —Psalm 8:4

My grandmother lived in an enormous white house; it seemed like a mansion. A pillared porch faced a large front yard. The backyard was huge. Inside, the ceilings were high and the rooms spacious.

Years later, my mother took me back to Grandmother's house. How shocked I was to discover how ordinary it was. The porch seemed tiny, and the front yard looked like a postage stamp. I could almost touch the ceilings. What was glorious to my childhood eyes seemed small and insig-

nificant through my adult eyes.

The psalmist describes the puniness of humans when measured against the grandeur of God's creation. Compared to the beauty of the heavens and the wonder of the moon and stars, we seem unimportant and ordinary.

Yet God loves us and has graced us richly, placing the whole creation at our feet. The psalmist marvels that God would even notice creatures, let alone crown them with glory and honor.

We humans may seem like nothing when viewed from the perspective of a vast creation. But in God's eyes, we are special—indeed, glorious. –Ron Adams

God, help me to see myself, and everyone I meet this day, from your perspective.

* * * * * * * * * * * * * * *

Devotional 5

What are human beings that you are mindful of them? —Psalm 8:4

When I was young, I often looked at the stars and viewed the majesty of God's vast creation. This verse resonates with what I felt back then—and occasionally today too.

The grand night sky puts me in touch with how minor my problems are and how very small we are. But given God's great glory and power, why is God so mindful of humans? We are even made "a little lower than God" (v. 5).

I now look at the heavens to remember how small I and my problems are in the greatness of God's creation and to keep in mind that God has crowned humans "with glory and honor" (v. 5).

This psalm teaches the importance of worship. It puts us in touch with God's glory and our glory. Worship helps us not to get down on ourselves. It encourages us to live up to the image in which we are made, to practice proper "dominion over the works of [God's] hands" (v. 6). God embraces both our smallness and our greatness. And so should we. −*Gordon Houser*

O God, how majestic is your name in all the earth!

* * * * * * * * * * * * * *

Devotional 6

You have made [human beings] a little lower than God, and crowned them with glory and honor. —Psalm 8:5

King George V once visited a British china factory. While viewing the delicate dishes, he picked up a saucer that had not fully dried, leaving his thumbprint on it. That unique piece gained enormous worth because of the imprint of the king.

God's royal imprint is on each human. At times we doubt our worth in the vastness and grandeur of the universe. Of what significance are humans in God's cosmos (v. 4)? The answer: The heavenly bodies, while magnificent, are a reflection of the Creator's beauty and power; they are not godlike. Yet people are godlike, created "a little lower than God" and "crowned . . . with glory and honor."

Humans are the summit of God's creation. When you are tempted to feel worthless, remember that imprint. Recall how valuable you are to God, who truly cares for you.

I bear the image of God, but so does my neighbor. I must treat each person with the dignity and respect an image bearer of God deserves. C. S. Lewis once said, "There are no ordinary people. You have never talked to a mere mortal." −*Walter Unger*

Help me to treat everyone I meet today with the respect an image bearer of God deserves.

* * * * * * * * * * * * * *

Devotional 7

O Lord, our Sovereign, how majestic is your name in all the earth! —Psalm 8:9

I listen for the songs of birds when I walk the woods. Crows caw overhead. A red-eyed vireo sings, "Hear me, see me, here I am." I see the flash of red of a cardinal.

Tall pines mix their green needles with the leaves of deciduous trees. I smell the earth with its rich dampness. A soft breeze caresses my face. I am caught in a warm summer shower. Wild blackberries are ready to eat.

In my walk, the wonders of creation activate my senses. As I savor and marvel at God's creation, I grow to love the Creator more.

To a workshop on creation near a city center, I took a handful of wildflowers from the countryside. I didn't think I would find plants in the city, but I found them in the cracks of the sidewalk and next to tall buildings. Birds flew from buildings to treetops. The sun and moon shone brightly. All were telling the glory of God. −*Jocele T. Meyer*

Creator God, all that is beneath the sun and in the heavens is full of your creative blessing. May we care for all, giving glory to you, our Maker.

God's glory in creation and the law

PSALM 19

Opening

Psalm 19 says that the ordinances of the Lord are sweeter than honey. Dip a finger in a bowl of honey, and savor its sweetness. What in your life has been sweet this week? What wasn't as sweet as you had hoped? Take time to share your reflections on this question and to check in with each other about what happened in the past week.

Understanding God's Word

About Psalm 19, C. S. Lewis wrote, "I take this to be the greatest poem in the Psalter and one of the greatest lyrics in the world."[1] Lewis, like most readers, puzzled over the relationship between the first six verses—a gorgeous hymn to the glory of God as it is "declared" by "his handiwork"—and the last eight verses—a hymn to the law and a prayer that the speaker of the psalm would be able to obey it and to worship in a way pleasing to God. Lewis eventually saw the connection, as most careful readers do, and with it the beauty and truth that shines from this psalm.

* *

For the leader

Bring a bowl of honey.

1. Pray for one another, naming aloud any prayer concerns, or sing a gathering song.

2. Read Psalm 19 aloud together. Take turns reading verses as you go around the group, or have one person read aloud the whole psalm while others close their eyes and listen.

---

1 C. S. Lewis, *Reflections on the Psalms* (New York: Harcourt, Brace and World, 1958), 63.

Psalm 19

Connecting with God's Word

Two parts, one psalm

Psalm 19's two parts—the Creation hymn (vv. 1-6) and the Torah hymn and prayer (vv. 7-14)—at first seem hard to hold together in a single psalm. However, they represent the two primary ways human beings can know God.

One way is through creation, the natural world. Although some Christians object to this idea as unbiblical, it is quite explicit here: the works of God declare without speech God's voice and God's glory.

The second way of knowing God is through Scripture, miracles, or direct communication from God to humans. This is the revelation celebrated in the final eight verses. The commandments—God's law or Torah—are not a collection of burdensome rules followed grimly and unsuccessfully. Instead, they are, like nature, a thing of delight and beauty, a gift from God.

The psalm ends with one of the great prayers of the Bible (v. 14). Words and heart, expression and motivation, are all subject to God's sight. But the God to whom the worshipper offers these words is neither distant nor disinterested. God is "my rock," the firm and dependable foundation beneath, and "my redeemer," the one in the entire world that can be counted on to take my side and to uphold my well-being.

- If nature speaks about God, what does it say? What are its limitations as a way of knowing God?

- What part of the Bible do you regard as your primary instruction manual? How does your understanding of Jesus Christ affect your understandings and attitudes toward the commandments of God?

- Have you ever felt that God was your "rock" or felt that God was your sure foundation? Share about those times.

Law and fear

The law is an ordering principle for protection in our daily lives, so we can live meaningfully. Think of *law* in terms of the Old Testament commandments and the five books of Moses (Torah) as interpreted in the life and teachings of Jesus. Reflect on Jesus' obedience to God and his willingness to apply the spirit of the law in ways not shared by the teachers of the law. What examples can you name?

The phrase "fear of the Lord" (v. 9) means different things to different people. Remember Moses' closing message to the children of Israel, related to hearing the law and learning to fear the Lord their God in Deuteronomy 31:13. Or Proverbs 9:10a: "The fear of the Lord is the beginning of wisdom." Or ponder Ecclesiastes 12:13b: "Fear God, and keep his commandments, for this is the duty of every human being."

The comparison of one Scripture text with another is foundational to all Bible study. Skim Psalm 103 and ponder a few key verses on the Lord's love to balance the emphasis in Psalm 19 on the law of the Lord and the fear of the Lord.

- What are the precepts or laws that guide your life? How are they different from or similar to the ones in Psalm 19?

- Why do you think the writer didn't include fear in the list of words to describe God's law, but instead used positive words such as *perfect, refreshing, sure,* and *right*?

- What does the phrase "fear of the Lord" mean to you? Have you ever experienced the fear of the Lord in your own life, in the past or in the present?

Living out the vision
In our world, religious bodies have different interpretations of the topics of law, fear, and sin. For followers of Jesus who pray, "Your kingdom come, your will be done" (Matthew 6:10), the stories of the beginning of the church in Acts are exemplary. When the Sanhedrin called Peter to appear before the council, he chose to obey God rather than the law (Acts 4:19-20), prayed for greater boldness in speaking the word of God (4:29), and confronted sin (5:1-11).

The message of Psalm 19 is no less emphatic: pleasing God requires a total commitment to God and God's law of love as revealed in Jesus Christ. It is this law, the fullest expression of the perfect law of the Lord, that is embodied in Jesus' claim to be the way-truth-life for all people (John 14:6).

- At what times in life have you felt fully committed to God and God's law of love? At what times has it been hard to feel committed?

- How does your understanding of Jesus Christ affect your understandings and attitudes toward God's commandments?

- Does following the law of the Lord seem freeing to you? Or does it seem restrictive? Why?

Closing

1. Name one way you see God's Word as sweet.

2. Close by reading slowly and prayerfully Psalm 103:2, 11:

   Bless the Lord, O my soul, and do not forget all his benefits.
   For as the heavens are high above the earth,
   so great is [your] steadfast love toward those who fear [you].

Devotionals

* * * * * * * * * * * * * * * * * *

Devotional 1

Let the words of my mouth and the meditation of my heart be acceptable to you, O LORD, my rock and my redeemer.
—Psalm 19:14

Recently I received an email from a co-worker about a certain topic. His response felt like a sharp rebuke. It was at the end of the day, and I was tired. I reacted poorly by explaining in a less-than-gracious tone that I clearly understood the policy. While both of us were irritable, we managed to come to some resolution.

The psalmist contemplates the sweet, life-giving words of God's law and then prays that his own thoughts and words may honor God. When I speak too quickly or when I am too weary to assess a situation carefully, I tend to speak words that I later regret. In my contact with my colleague, no great harm was done, but my testiness reminded me of my desire to speak words and think thoughts that are acceptable to God. —Teresa Moser

Listening God, you know all my words and thoughts. Teach me to speak carefully so that my words are as sweet to you as your words are to me.

* * * * * * * * * * * * * * *

Devotional 2

The heavens are telling the glory of God.
—Psalm 19:1

With the exception of farmers, construction workers, park employees, and a few others, most of us spend little time outside. Consequently, we tend to ignore the natural world, except when it bothers us (it's raining, it's too hot, I'd better bundle up). Or we may romanticize it, gazing at pictures of beautiful mountains or sunsets.

Ancient peoples, however, spent most of their time outside. They understood the power of nature to destroy or to produce life. They saw themselves as a part of and subject to a larger world, not as being in control of it.

Our consumerist culture, on the other hand, tends to see nature as merely something to use. We don't always respect its limits or its warnings until we lose our houses through floods or earthquakes. Let's look up and learn from the heavens about God's glory. —Gordon Houser

We marvel at your handiwork, O God, and we praise you.

* * * * * * * * * * * * * *

Devotional 3

By them is your servant warned; in keeping them there is great reward. —Psalm 19:11

I spent a few days in Victoria, B.C., observing the inner harbor where floatplanes occasionally landed and took off, right in the center of the city. Ferries and helicopters also came and went in that space, along with private vessels.

It struck me how important a flight plan would be in that harbor area. Clear guidelines for where a floatplane would go once it became airborne would be critical. The pilot would have to fly according to strict rules.

As Christians, we live by the new covenant: the way of the cross. That means our flight plan follows the markers of practicing sacrifice and submission, living by the Spirit, abiding in Christ, and walking according to his example as God enables us to do so. And in so doing, we are promised great reward. –David Wiebe

Master Pilot, we depend on you for directions and for the path to follow. Help us to stick to the plan you have set out for us. And lead us to life everlasting.

* * * * * * * * * * * * * *

Devotional 4

More to be desired are they than gold, even much fine gold; sweeter also than honey, and drippings of the honeycomb. —Psalm 19:10

In our Bible study group, we would sing the words of this psalm accompanied by a guitar. Following the descriptions of the "law of the Lord" came the refrain, "More to be desired are they than gold, even much fine gold: sweeter also than honey and the honeycomb." Verse 11 was the coda: "Moreover by them is your servant warned; in keeping of them there is great reward."

The tune and the rhythm made it easy to sing without considering the meaning of the words. Now I'm taking a closer look.

Personally, I need the wisdom, joy, and guidance that God's Word provides. I need to remind myself of the refrain so that the words of Psalm 19:10 are etched in my mind. But I want them to go beyond my mind and be evident in my life. I continually need to rediscover how sweet and precious God's Word is. –Lydia Siemens Harris

Forgive me, Lord, for the times that I neglect your Word. Grant me a daily desire to savor its sweetness and valuable truths.

* * * * * * * * * * * * * *

Devotional 5

The precepts of the Lord are right, rejoicing the heart. —Psalm 19:8

My husband's comment after a meaningful devotional, Scripture reading, or hearty meal is often "good stuff!" His enthusiastic tone of voice speaks of genuine satisfaction and enjoyment—a need met, an appetite well filled. Whether it is a physical hunger or a spiritual yearning, I know by that tone and the look in his eyes that he has found deep delight in having the sustenance "hit the spot."

That is the way God's Word is to us. Finding a verse that is just what we need at the moment is a miraculous and satisfying surprise that brings true delight in God's goodness.

Today's Scripture names some ways the Word fills our needs. It revives the soul, makes wise the simple, rejoices the heart, and enlightens the eyes. God's pure and enduring word is more precious than fine gold, sweeter than honey. Ah! It is "good stuff" indeed! –Ruth Smith Meyer

Today, "Let the words of my mouth and the meditation of my heart be acceptable to you, O Lord, my rock and my redeemer" (v. 14).

* * * * * * * * * * * * * * *

Devotional 6

[The sun's] rising is from the end of the heavens, and its circuit to the end of them; and nothing is hid from its heat. —Psalm 19:6

When the sun hides behind clouds for days on end, it is like truth remaining hidden. Just as humankind can look back to commonly held beliefs of centuries ago that we know to be different today, each of us can also look back on beliefs or decisions from earlier in life and say, "If only I had known then what I know now." But all the facts and implications of our actions are never clear to us at the time. Only God can see the complete picture of past, present, and future.

The psalmist suggests that just as nothing is hidden from the sun, nothing in our lives is hidden from God. May God's presence in our lives give light and heat to all corners of the earth. *—Amy Dueckman*

O God, your light shines into all the corners of my life. May both the words I speak and the inner workings of my heart be acceptable in your sight.

* * * * * * * * * * * * * * *

Devotional 7

The heavens are telling the glory of God; and the firmament proclaims his handiwork. —Psalm 19:1

By the end of January in Pennsylvania, I begin to feel claustrophobic. I start to miss the effects of nature's vitamin D. The sunshine does brighten my spirits as I look at it from the windows, but I miss the direct contact of leisurely summer picnics and coffee by the pond.

My coping strategy on my way to work, therefore, is to turn off the music, turn the heat up to full blast, and open my window. Immediately, I'm in a different world. I can hear birds I forgot were out there. The air smells clean. Clouds are whiter.

Into these moments come today's words from the psalmist: "The heavens are telling the glory of God; and the firmament proclaims his handiwork." The world is busy with the job for which it was created: being a witness to the glory of God. *—Sandra Drescher-Lehman*

God, as we bring indoors something from outside, you remind us that your glory speaks in the world at all times, and sometimes without words.

God's comfort and reassurance

PSALM 23

* *

Opening

Psalm 23 offers comfort and reassurance that God cares about us and is willing and able to meet our needs, whether spiritual, physical, psychological, or material. Invite each group member to feel a sheepskin or wool blanket. Then think about times you felt God's comfort in your daily life.

Understanding God's Word

Shepherding was not a prestigious occupation in the Ancient Near East. Shepherds spent a lot of time alone. They often cared for sheep belonging to their extended family or for their neighbors. Shepherds led the sheep to water and vegetation, and they protected them from predators, both animal and human. Sometimes shepherds traveled long distances to meet the needs of the sheep.

Connecting with God's Word

A psalm of David

This psalm is titled "A psalm of David." In Hebrew, some words can have several meanings. This superscription may mean that the psalm was written by

* *

For the leader

Bring a sheepskin or wool blanket.

1. In a season of prayer, thank God for the strength and comfort you, your family, and/or your congregation has received for specific situations and needs.

2. Recite Psalm 23 together as your confession of faith in and thanksgiving for God's comforting care.

David, for David, or in honor of David. It could also mean that it was written in the style of David. It is therefore not clear that David actually wrote the psalm, even though we know he was a shepherd as a young man.

The shepherd: A sheep's eye view (23:1-6)
This psalm reflects on the shepherd from the point of view of the sheep. The sheep are comforted by the fact that Yahweh, as shepherd, meets all their needs. Their specific needs include food, water, guidance on the right road, and protection from harm. The rod and staff (v. 4) are not instruments of punishment but are used to guide the sheep and protect them from predators.

In Hebrew, which was written without vowels, the Lord's name appears as four Hebrew letters (sometimes written as YHWH in English). In this psalm, the use of YHWH stresses that the God of Israel, not just any god, is the One who provides for his people.

Yahweh the host (23:5-6)
Verse 5 marks a shift from the sheep imagery to host/guest imagery. The Lord is the host and has set a lavish table for welcomed guests. Anointing with oil is a symbol of honor, often afforded special guests in the Ancient Near East. The enemies may be social or political enemies rather than military enemies. In verse 6, the virtues of goodness and mercy "follow" the psalmist. A more accurate translation is that these virtues pursue the poet actively and deliberately.

Living out the vision
This psalm is a favorite because it offers comfort and reassurance that God cares about us and is willing and able to meet our needs, whether spiritual, physical, psychological, or material. Lifting our eyes to the hills does not change realities on the ground, but it does give us a different perspective.

- At what times have you felt God's comfort and reassurance in the last month? Describe two of these times in writing. Share with other members of the study group.

- On what occasions have you gained a new perspective for a situation you confronted in the last month? With other members of the study group, share your experience, the new insights gained, and how it affected your attitude or behavior.

Some images used in Psalm 23, such as the picture of grazing sheep, may not be part of our daily lives. As a result, we may misinterpret the meaning of the psalm. When I was a child, I imagined the shepherd frolicking happily with the sheep when not napping under a shady tree. I never thought about the real work and danger involved in the occupation. Those who live in towns or cities of some size are far removed from the scenes envisioned in this psalm.

- What metaphor from your everyday life conveys the idea that there is one who provides for life needs, restores your soul, and is present in the shadow of death?

- Write a contemporary psalm in your own words that expresses the same thoughts as Psalm 23.

This psalm assures us that the Shepherd will lead us on "right paths" and "through dark valleys, and host us "in the presence of [our] enemies" (vv. 3-5).

- Reflect on those occasions when you felt the Shepherd leading you through difficult circumstances. What crisis did you face, and how did the Shepherd lead you through it? Share one event with the members of your study group. How have members of the group helped you move through these events?

- Does following the Shepherd make life easier for you? How has the quality of your spiritual life been enriched through your relationship to the Shepherd?

- How have you expressed your thanks and praise to the Shepherd for his careful and life-giving leading?

Sometimes bad things happen to good people. We likely have heard of people who left the church because some harm came to them or someone they loved. Perhaps a child was injured in a car accident. Maybe a breadwinner lost a job, or a friend became an enemy. Perhaps a spouse asked for a divorce.

- How do you explain such negative events in light of the assurance that God's goodness and mercy follows us all our days (v. 6)?

Closing

1. Describe one way God has comforted and strengthened you. Offer thanks to God for such loving care.

2. Pray for one another that each may be empowered to meet any life crisis that may come before the study group meets again.

3. Close the session by reciting Psalm 23 from memory or invite one group member to share the psalm written in contemporary imagery.

* * * * * * * * * * * * * * * * *

Devotional 1

The LORD is my Shepherd, I shall not want.
—Psalm 23:1

In their ministry, Jason and Amy served in an impoverished country. Their van was used to help others by taking them to school, to a hospital, or to visit family. When their van broke down, they faced a crisis. They had no way to visit their daughter, who lived two hours away.

The van repair estimate was $250, all the money they had available. While the van was being fixed, a friend needed that amount of money. Jason wanted to help, but could he delay payment for the van repair? He presented this matter to God.

Jason gave away the $250 without knowing how to pay for the van repairs. On the day the van was fixed, Jason and Amy received a letter with a donation of $250 enclosed.

When we trust God for our needs, we can minister freely to others. Jesus, our Good Shepherd, modeled the way by giving his life for us. He trusted in God's promise of new life for all. *–Melissa Glauser*

Father, give me faith in your provision and sensitivity to your Spirit's nudging, so I can cheerfully give to others.

* * * * * * * * * * * * * *

Devotional 2

The LORD is my shepherd, I shall not want. He makes me lie down in green pastures; he leads me beside still waters. —Psalm 23:1-2

"Psalm 23 is about God's abundance," explained our tour guide on the parched Judean hills. Neither green grass nor water was in sight. Sheep searched for food among brown, dry stalks. "The sheep don't lift their heads lest their noses miss finding their lunch of small pods of seeds." How did this relate to Psalm 23?

Shepherds led their sheep to find food. In the dry season, water was hard to find. In the rainy season, sheep feared water that swirled around rocks in the streambeds. In other seasons, shepherds imagined pools of still water that sheep liked and pastures with lush green grass in which they could lie down and rest. Such abundance!

David–shepherd, psalmist, and poet– thought of the God of abundance. Beyond food and water, there is safety, comfort, freedom from fear, companionship, a heavenly banquet, and an eternal home with the Lord as host. Could anyone want more? *–Ferne Burkhardt*

Lord, forgive me for taking for granted the abundance of gifts you shower on me. Accept my thanks today.

* * * * * * * * * * * * * *

Devotional 3

The LORD is my shepherd. . . . He restores my soul. He leads me in right paths for his name's sake. —Psalm 23:1, 3

These words and pictures offer clear promises to people in challenging circumstances. By repeating and memorizing this psalm, many have experienced God's guidance.

Some time ago, the president of a large corporation called me to his office to pray with him. He was facing uncertainty on several fronts. Union encroachment, provincial regulations, succession planning, and expansion were his daily challenges. "In my wildest dreams," he said, "I never expected to be this successful. Neither did I expect the tremendous challenges for the future."

He had asked me to come, not because I could speak to these issues, but because he wanted to make a promise "out loud" to God. He promised to continue to live by the principles of equity, fairness, and trust. Then he asked me for biblical phrases that would encourage his promise. I suggested, "Each day, before you begin your work, repeat Psalm 23." Sometime later, he called to say, "It is working for me." *–Doug Snyder*

Each day, Lord, I affirm your care for me, your provision of good, and your presence—even in the most difficult decisions I must make.

* * * * * * * * * * * * * *

Devotional 4

[The Lord] restores my soul. He leads me in right paths for his name's sake. —Psalm 23:3

In Psalm 23, David speaks as a sheep that trusts the shepherd implicitly and follows without fear.

I have had many opportunities to trust God. As complex decisions loom before me, I give myself over to God's leading–but with fear and trembling. One decision that caused much anxiety was our move from Ontario to Manitoba to be near our family. It meant uprooting from our home, our friends, and our church family of over twenty years.

While we approached this move with prayer and planning, anxiety still gripped us. Our answer to prayer was that our house sold much sooner than we had expected. Packing had to be accelerated; we had to find another house; and we had to move in winter. As I look back, I see our Shepherd's hand guiding us all the way.

Psalm 23 reminds me that in the midst of the turbulence of life, I need to relax in God's presence and follow while he leads. *–Elfrieda Neufeld Schroeder*

Jesus, gentle Shepherd, you know the way. Help me not to follow you anxiously, but in complete trust.

* * * * * * * * * * * * * *

Devotional 5

Even though I walk through the valley of the shadow of death, I fear no evil, for you are with me. —Psalm 23:4

A young woman, widowed as a result of the September 11, 2001, terrorist attacks, related the horrifying events of that morning and the grief-filled months that followed. She testified that her faith in God and the comforting knowledge that her husband was in God's presence kept her going.

Raising three young children without their father presented challenges she could hardly bear. Yet she remained confident that God would supply everything her family needed.

While many have not had to deal with a tragedy like the one this woman faced, fears, illness, and death visit all of us. Psalm 23 is as true today as when it was first penned. Like a shepherd that cares for sheep, God tenderly watches over us. The Lord walks with us, provides physical necessities, and meets our emotional and spiritual needs.

Are you wandering through a dark valley? Has fear invaded your mind and paralyzed your spirit? Reach out to the hand of the Shepherd. Allow the Lord to guide you, comfort you, and lovingly care for you. *–Nancy Witmer*

Lord, I cling to the promise that you will walk with me through every day of my life. Thank you for your faithful care.

Devotional 6

You prepare a table before me. . . . you anoint my head with oil. —Psalm 23:5

God enters this psalm as a Bedouin shepherd but exits as a desert sheik in the role of host. The opening metaphor of flock and shepherd is familiar, but the subtle shift toward the image of guest and magnanimous host is less memorable.

That God will lavishly host us is fully in accord with Jesus' picture ("In my Father's house are many rooms," John 14:2 *NIV*) and with the sweeping mural of the Lamb's marriage supper in John's Revelation (19:6-9).

This movement within the psalm and across the whole salvation story underscores how close hospitality is to the heart of good news. This "table" stands as a modest but powerful sign of God's presence and purpose in the world.

Our tables should help make the coming banquet present now for our neighbors. Might we collectively baptize our tables and devote them to imitate God's great work—to lay a never-to-be-forgotten and not-to-be-missed feast for the peoples of the world? *–Jonathan Larson*

Thy hand, in sight of all my foes, doth still my table spread. My cup with blessings overflows, thine oil anoints my head (Isaac Watts).

Devotional 7

Surely goodness and mercy shall follow me all the days of my life, and I shall dwell in the house of the LORD my whole life long. —Psalm 23:6

David believed that goodness and mercy would "follow" him. How do our actions and attributes "follow" us? Our deeds, whether good or evil, kind or inconsiderate, form the reputation that follows us.

Whatever goodness follows us is ultimately God's. While David's life was far from perfect, he stated this text with full confidence. How could he be so sure of his status with God? David's confidence was likely rooted in the grace God showed him as he confronted his sin in Psalm 51. David repented and trusted God to "restore [his] soul" (23:3).

We can have that same confidence when we repent of our sins, claim God's forgiveness, and choose to follow the Lord. The legacy of the psalms continues to direct us to praise God and celebrate his goodness.

What kind of reputation and legacy follow you? Do you leave a trail of goodness and mercy? Does your life show that you trust the Good Shepherd to lead you in paths of righteousness? *–Susan Miller Balzer*

Lord, may goodness and mercy follow me as I, with your grace and guidance, follow in your steps, my Savior and Shepherd.

Joy in forgiveness

* *

Opening

Psalm 32 is a testimony of a writer who had sinned and found forgiveness after confessing his wrongdoing to the Lord. What is your experience of sin against and forgiveness from God? Have you sinned against another person and received forgiveness? How did this experience change your relationships? Did the ritual of confession and forgiveness of sin help you find forgiveness?

Understanding God's Word

Psalm 32 is sometimes considered a Wisdom psalm because of the admonitions that appear in verses 8-11. Like Psalm 1, it begins with the word *happy* (some translations use *blessed*) and a description of who is happy. It has also been called a psalm of thanksgiving because the psalmist expresses appreciation for what God has done.

This psalm may be considered a testimony. In testimonies, individuals tell their own stories and then encourage listeners to learn from their example. The testimony here lacks specific details of the poet's experience. Nevertheless, the poet tells a story of pain that is turned around when he or she confesses sin to God.

* *

For the leader

Ask your pastor for a book or collection of worship resources. Examine the ritual of confession and forgiveness of sin. Become familiar with the way this is done in your congregation.

1. Offer prayers of thanksgiving and praise to God for the way members of the group have experienced forgiveness from God and other people.

2. Read Psalm 32. Assign the responsive reading as follows: verses 1-4 in unison; 5 one reader; 6-7 another reader; 8-11 in unison.

Note that the word *selah* appears after verses 4, 5, and 7. The meaning of this word is unclear, although some suggest that it may mark a place where a musical interlude could be played or it may indicate a pause or a place where a solo voice spoke. Each time *selah* appears, the direction of the poet's thoughts changes.

Connecting with God's Word

The benefits of confession (32:3-5)
These verses are stated in the first person (I, my). The psalmist noticed that his unconfessed sin had a physical effect on his body: "When I kept silent, my bones wasted away . . . my strength was sapped" (vv. 3-4 *NIV*). It is only by the grace of God that we are sensitive to our own guilt. Being aware of sin and being affected by it is a sign of God's presence, not God's absence. The psalmist recognized this by saying, "Your hand was heavy upon me" (v. 4). God's intense presence results in what God wants: the psalmist's confession to the Lord. It is not the wrath of God that rains down on the confessor but the healing balm of God's forgiveness.

- When you become aware of sin in your life, how and to whom do you confess your error? Do you speak privately with God? Do you contact a close confidant?

- Some church bodies include confession as a part of every weekly worship service. Usually a general prayer of confession is read in unison or responsively, or the worship leader prays on behalf of the congregation. The confession is followed by a word of forgiveness, an assurance of the forgiveness of sins.

How is confession handled in your congregation? Is it public? Private? Is it made to God? To the person sinned against? To the pastor or elders? To friends? Is it necessary or helpful to confess your sins only to God?

Good advice (32:6-7)
The psalmist calls out to everyone who is "faithful." The Hebrew word for "faithful" is hasid, defined as the characteristic of "one who does kind things." The admonition to these faithful is that they should pray so that they can experience God's protection and deliverance.

Verse 7 is one of several that describe God as a hiding place or one who provides a hiding place. This imagery likely reflects the harsh reality in the Ancient Near East. There were no police forces in Canaan. Ordinary people had to defend themselves alone or band together as a family, clan, or tribe. Hiding was an option for self-protection (see 1 Samuel 13:6)—and a nonviolent one at that. In this psalm, trouble of a variety of kinds is envisioned. God will protect the faithful from any type of trouble.

- The hiding place is a place of protection, rest, and renovation. Some people hide in plain sight. After the last exams are in, one teacher I know disappears from campus. She grades the exams at an out-of-the-way coffee shop. Being off campus, she is not constantly interrupted by students who ask whether their grades are finished.

  From what do you find yourself most in need of protection? Where are your hiding places? If you do not have one, where would you like to create one?

- During severe weather, community leaders advise residents to go to (hiding) places where they can be safe. Where do you go when these alerts sound? Do you make sure vulnerable family members and neighbors are provided with safe places? Do you pray for the safekeeping of others? If tragedy occurs, do you help locate and check in on those whose "hiding" places have been damaged or destroyed? Is your church building available to host those who cannot return to their homes or businesses?

Words of advice (32:8-11)

The psalmist changes the audience from God to the people, saying that they should not be like horses or mules whose guidance is from outside. To be instructed is to gain knowledge and insight to guide oneself.

Notice that the sinner in this case is also the faithful one. This psalm does not address those who do not know God and do not care about what God wants, but those whose consciences are active and who long for God.

The psalmist warns the listener that the torments of the wicked are many. But the love of God surrounds those who trust God. Joy and love are gifts to them.

- How comfortable are you in sharing your experience of God with others? Do you tend to focus only on "successes," or are you willing also to share your failures and what you learned from them?

- Discuss whether you should share the psalmist's counsel with unbelievers. If so, brainstorm ways this could be done as part of your congregation's outreach.

Closing

1. Give testimony to a personal experience of being loved by God after you were forgiven of sin.

2. Close by repeating Psalm 32 in the manner in which it was presented at the beginning of this session.

DEVOTIONALS

Devotional 1

Happy are those whose transgression is forgiven, whose sin is covered. —Psalm 32:1

In Psalm 32, the psalmist voices the need for repentance. When he stops covering up his wrongdoings, God extends a cover of forgiveness over his sins. The joy of being forgiven sparkles throughout the psalm.

As a new mom, I breathe a sigh of relief. Often weary and sleep deprived from chasing after my ultra-active one year old, I easily lose my patience. The stacks of laundry, toys, dirty diapers, and crumbs wear me down. Many nights I confess, "God, I could have been a more patient mom today. Please forgive me. Grant me the energy to change." As I pour out my heart to God, a sense of peace and forgiveness washes over me.

God grants me the joy of a fresh start as I wake refreshed the next morning, eager to greet the smiling little face that peers out at me from his crib. I pray that, God willing, the patience I lacked yesterday will be mine today. *–Julie Ellison White*

Lord, so often I fail to measure up to your expectations; my faults are numerous. Help me to know the joy of a fresh start that results from your forgiveness.

Devotional 2

Happy are those whose transgression is forgiven, whose sin is covered. —Psalm 32:1

"Will you forgive me?" my husband asked after one of our heated "discussions." I stiffened and didn't reply. "He doesn't deserve it," I thought. But I knew it took courage and humility for him to ask forgiveness. Although I didn't feel like it, I remembered God forgave me when I didn't deserve it (Romans 5:8). My heart softened, and I replied, "Yes, dear, I forgive you. Will you forgive me?" It felt wonderful to forgive and be forgiven.

Forgiveness is essential for all relationships, with God and others. When our engaged son asked family and friends for marriage advice, I said, "Be quick to forgive and ask forgiveness. Then you'll reap peace and joy in your marriage." I knew it was good advice. I'd tested it for thirty-two years.

During the Lenten season, we recall that our forgiveness came at a great price to God—the death of his dear son, Jesus. How blessed and happy we are to be forgiven. *–Lydia E. Harris*

Gracious God, thank you for forgiving my sins. Help me forgive others the way you have forgiven me.

* * * * * * * * * * * * * * *

Devotional 3

My strength was dried up as by the heat of summer. —Psalm 32:4

Psalm 32 is viewed as David's response to the whole Bathsheba debacle, recorded in 2 Samuel 11. When he becomes aware of the magnitude of his wrongdoing, he slides into the hot seat with God. With beads of sweat hanging on his brow, he tosses and turns in agony as he tries to quiet himself.

Then he confesses his wrongdoing to the Lord, and the air suddenly cools. The burning summer heat of sin is replaced by the cool wind of God's Spirit. Joy and excitement pour out as his confession provides release and refuge.

When David was first anointed king, God told Samuel, "The Lord does not see as mortals see; they look on the outward appearance, but the Lord looks on the heart" (1 Samuel 16:7). This willingness to confess must have been one of the attributes God saw when he looked within David's heart. Can the same be said of you, of me? *–Tyler Hartford*

Search me, O God, and know my heart; test me and know my thoughts. See if there is any wicked way in me, and lead me in the way everlasting (Psalm 139:23-24).

* * * * * * * * * * * * * * *

Devotional 4

I said, "I will confess my transgressions to the Lord," and you forgave the guilt of my sin. —Psalm 32:5

The room was still; even babies seemed to know this was a sacred moment. I had invited members to write down one grievance they were willing to release. Writing it meant they were agreeing to ask for God's forgiveness and for the strength to move beyond the power this grievance held.

After the writing, I asked those able and willing to bring their slips to a table at the front and place them in a basket. Scores of folks arose from their pews and responded. We then proceeded outside and burned the slips in the church parking lot.

It's hard to describe the power of this service of forgiveness. Most everyone took part. There was a visible display of emotion. I was surprised by the impact of this ritual, but I shouldn't have been. This psalm affirms the power of letting go through confession and going forward with God. *–Larry Hauder*

God of forgiveness, stand with me today as I seek to release grudges I've harbored.

* * * * * * * * * * * * * * *

Devotional 5

You are a hiding place for me; you preserve me from trouble; you surround me with glad cries of deliverance. —Psalm 32:7

When my youngest son was small, he loved to curl up in one of the floor-level kitchen cupboards. He would take out the cereal boxes and turn the cupboard into his own little nest. One of my favorite photos of him is in that space with a look of perfect delight and satisfaction on his face. He was safe and content.

But life is not free of pain and sorrow, even though we often pretend it is. During times of trouble, I have learned that hiding my circumstances and pretending that all is well does not let me draw from the healing power of community or find safety in the arms of a loving God.

The psalmist knew better. Just as there is no hiding place from trouble, there is no hiding place from God. Just as young children seek out small, quiet nests, we can seek the shelter of God's hiding place. From there we can rest our eyes, calm our ragged breathing, and be renewed. –*Regina Shands Stoltzfus*

Gracious God, you are my safe place. In times of trouble, I will run to you. Thank you for accepting me just as I come.

* * * * * * * * * * * * * * *

Devotional 6

I will instruct and teach you the way you should go; I will counsel you with my eye upon you. —Psalm 32:8

Eye contact is very important in communicating with animals. Animal trainers stress the necessity of keeping one's eyes on them, because they are most proficient in nonverbal language. My ten-year-old collie has a steady, intent gaze when he's watching for a tasty crumb to drop from my fingers. But when he's guilty of misbehavior, he drops his head and refuses to meet my eyes.

Nonverbal language is also very important to people. Such messages can account for 90 percent of all communication, and the eyes are at the center of it. Consider exchanges you've had with others recently. Did you see love and warmth in his eyes? Were her eyes guarded or fearful?

The psalmist sees God as a teacher with a watchful eye, carefully guiding our steps. Confessing our shortcomings frees us to receive God's forgiveness and protection. While it may take time to learn the value of honest acknowledgment, God's eye is instructing and counseling us. –*Melissa Miller*

Wise Teacher, I need your guidance; I am too often without understanding. Keep me near you.

* * * * * * * * * * * * * * *

Devotional 7

Do not be like a horse or a mule, without understanding, whose temper must be curbed with bit and bridle, else it will not stay near you. —Psalm 32:9

Nature teaches powerful lessons. This passage highlights the lack of "understanding" among horses and mules. Bumblebees can also appear rather ignorant. A bumblebee can die if it finds itself at the bottom of an open tumbler. It cannot sense that the way of escape is at the top. Unless liberated from above, the bumblebee will seek a way out where none exists until it destroys itself.

The psalmist was beating his head against a tumbler, as it were. He refused to submit to God and confess his burden (vv. 3-4). Finally, he acknowledged that the way out was the way up (v. 5). He quit covering up, submitted to God, and confessed his sin.

A strong temptation for many is to hide our sin. We're afraid we'll be embarrassed, lose face or lose our position in the church. And so we hold it in and suffer the physical consequences of our inner turmoil. But rejoicing and gladness come as we submit to God's plan. –*Dave Wiebe*

God, I'm a proud person. I resist submission to your way. Help me to yield my will to yours and find rest for my soul.

Tell the story

PSALM 78

Opening

Psalm 78:1-11 introduces the story of God's gracious actions in dealing with the people of Israel in spite of their rebellion and disobedience to the law and commandments given at Mount Sinai. It reflects the determination of the psalmist to tell the story of God's ways—as well as the people's responses—to the next generation.

Highlight family and the congregational histories. How have these stories been retold to the young and old? Do they know and appreciate them? What is the evidence that they have accepted these stories as their own? Have some rejected these stories and gone their own way?

For the leader

Bring family and congregational histories and artifacts.

1. Verses 12-32 describe the wilderness journey in which God's gracious acts were followed by Israel's rebellion and God's angry response. Verses 33-39 highlight God's restraint and compassion. Like verses 12-39, verses 40-64 recite the events that occurred from Egypt to Canaan with similar responses from the people as well as God's gracious activity and discipline. Verses 65-72 describe God's decision that Judah, Zion (Jerusalem), and King David would be the people and places that would receive divine priority in the future.

- What events and signs have you observed this week that show God's love and grace toward your community?

- What acts of rebellion and disobedience to God's ways have you seen?

- What responses of God's love and grace have you seen in the face of such rejection?

2. Read verses 1-16. Invite three group members to read as follows: verses 1-4; verses 5-8; and verses 9-16.

Understanding God's Word

Psalm 78, identified as a *maskil* of Asaph, is a bit difficult to classify. It is a kind of litany that reviews the history of Israel. Its purpose is to teach the people, especially the children, the things that God has done to provide hope and confidence to future generations. It affirms the leadership of David and the priority of the tribe of Judah. In this session, the focus is on verses 1-8.

Connecting with God's Word

A call to listen (78:1-4)

The poem opens with a voice asking people to listen to a lesson (v. 1). The voice is that of a teacher of wisdom, who identifies with the audience as one of them ("our ancestors," v. 3). These two sentences say the same thing. This common structure in Israelite poetry, called synonymous parallelism, is a way of reinforcing the point and aiding memory among the hearers.

In verse 2, the psalmist speaks "in a parable." But what the psalmist offers is not a parable or proverb; it is a review of Israel's history with a commentary.

In verses 3-4, the psalmist reminds the Israelites of the awesome things that God has done. They already know these things because their ancestors have passed the stories down. In verse 4, the psalmist states that these things will not be hidden from the children.

Why would anyone want to hide from children the things that God has done? Because one cannot recount what God has done in history without mentioning the way the ancestors responded to God's gracious acts—often with disobedience and ingratitude. But if the children and the children's children are to learn to place their hope in God, they must understand the whole story of how God was good to the ancestors.

Adults tell and interpret history to children. We tend to tell it in such a way that it makes us, or our side, look good. The Israelites chose to tell their shameful stories as well as their heroic stories so that their children would understand that God did what was right. When things went wrong, it was their failure, not God's.

- Reflect carefully on articles and presentations you have read or heard from government and other secular and religious leaders. Did they emphasize the positive and not report their failure to carry forward the work or mission that was their mandate?

- How do we explain our failure to act when we could have made a positive difference in the life of an individual or a community?

Do not forget (78:5-8)

The psalmist wants to make clear that it is God who has ordered the continued teaching of the ancestral stories. In an oral culture, such stories, knowledge, and wisdom can be lost in a single generation. Therefore, each generation is obliged to tell the next.

The parents are told to teach the next generation to observe God's commandments so that they may not be like their ancestors (v. 8). This is a significant twist. Rather than holding up the ancestors as role models, the children are told that they should not be like them. The ancestors provide a negative example. The remainder of the psalm lists the rebelliousness and disobedience of the ancestors in contrast to God's graciousness.

It is a mistake to think that all the Israelite ancestors were rebellious all the time. Creating a stark contrast is a frequently used teaching technique. If those ancestors were always rebellious, they would not have treasured and passed down the Scriptures.

- In immigrant communities, the generation that immigrated often wants to hold on to the traditions of the old country. The second or third generation wants to be free of the constraints of a culture and place with which they have no firsthand experience. But the third or fourth generation of the descendants of the immigrants may develop an interest in their origins and want to learn the culture of its ancestors.

    What has been the experience of your family and congregation: have parents prepared their stories for their children?

- The value of knowledge written or recorded is that if one generation is not interested, a subsequent generation can learn the knowledge, stories, and wisdom. Many congregations have an account of their history. If yours does not, you may want to begin to research and write the collected memories of members of the study group. Or you may want to encourage church leaders to arrange for its history to be prepared, perhaps for an anniversary celebration of its founding.

Closing

1. Recall one important memory from your congregation's history that continues to influence the life of your church community today. Or share a significant event that occurred in your family several years ago that continues to impact your life and faith.

2. Close by reading the first part of Psalm 78 as you did in the beginning of the session.

DEVOTIONALS

* *

Devotional 1

We will tell to the coming generation the glorious deeds of the LORD, and his might, and the wonders that he has done. —Psalm 78:4

As I was reading about those who shared the cup of cold water in the name of Jesus, I came upon a one-sentence reference to a missionary. In 1920, despite great danger to herself, one woman protected Armenian orphans during Turkey's great genocide.

I wanted to know more. The author didn't know any more details, but my research led me to a great-niece of this woman. She told me that the missionary had married later in life and had a living daughter. I contacted the daughter and heard a very exciting story. What did I do with this research? I used it for a children's story that I told in my congregation.

To me, there are few things in worship more important than the children's story. Here we tell the next generation that we are walking on the shoulders of giants—people who accomplished great things with the help of the Lord. If we don't tell our children the glorious deeds of the Lord, who will? —Frank Ramirez

God of story, call us to recount your glory as it is embodied in those who have lived the gospel.

* * * * * * * * * * * * * * *

Devotional 2

We will not hide them from their children; We will tell to the coming generation the glorious deeds of the LORD, and his might, and the wonders that he has done. —Psalm 78:4

While visiting a friend, I attended a church choir picnic. Though I had worshipped with this church once before and had met a few of the people, those around the table were mostly strangers.

They began telling stories about the congregation. Members in their sixties and seventies told of watching children grow through their teen years and into adulthood. They spoke of befriending, supporting, and ministering to people who had been part of their church family in earlier times but no longer attend—in hope that they would return to the faith community.

Sometimes such gatherings and conversations leave a guest feeling out of place. But as I listened, I felt I was hearing stories that belong to the whole church. When the psalmist speaks of telling God's goodness to the generations, it is not only about human family units or about a specific believing body. Stories of God's faithfulness are to be shared among God's people everywhere. —Teresa Moser

As I hear and tell the stories of God's faithfulness, I claim them as my own and give thanks for God's goodness.

* * * * * * * * * * * * * *

Devotional 3

We will tell to the coming generation the glorious deeds of the Lord. —Psalm 78:4

In the cities of Beijing and Xian, I saw monuments built to remind new generations of the glorious deeds of China's first emperor, Qin Shi Huang. He united the nation's warring factions; instituted uniform systems of writing, taxation, law, measurement, and money; and built roads.

Qin Shi Huang fostered national unity by building the Great Wall. Laborers sculpted eight thousand life-size terra-cotta soldiers to be buried in his tomb as a testament to his military might. I was awed by the glorious deeds of this great king.

The psalmist speaks of the importance of telling new generations of God's glorious deeds. Will we do that by building impressive architectural wonders as the ancient Chinese emperor did? No, our testament to God's greatness lies in the way we live and relate to those around us.

We honor our God when we imitate Jesus Christ daily. Godly living by Christians worldwide would bring about a change far greater than what Emperor Qin brought to China. —MaryLou Driedger

God, I want my daily actions to be a testament to your glorious deeds. I pledge to pass on your legacy of love and peace to coming generations and to the world.

* * * * * * * * * * * * * *

Devotional 4

They ate and were well filled, for he gave them what they craved. —Psalm 78:29

I love the long, hot days of summer—the profusion of plants and flowers, walking without shoes. I want it to last forever.

In the cold, gray days of February, I pine for the warm sun. But then a curious thing occurs. When I think I can't stand winter any longer, I'm surprised by a sunny day, with a whiff of spring fragrance. A crocus pokes through the still, cold ground. Green buds appear on the trees. The earth is coming back to life.

While I grumble about the cold, I enjoy living in a climate where the seasons are easily observed. While I love summer the most, I tend to take it for granted. Each year I am reminded of the rhythm of creation and God's order over all the earth. I experience new life; I understand a new resurrection. I find that I don't really crave perpetual summer; just knowing summer will return is enough. —Regina Shands Stoltzfus

Gracious God, you created the earth and all that is within it. You order the days and the seasons, and you feed us from earth's bounty. Thank you!

* * * * * * * * * * * * * *

Devotional 5

[The next generation] should not be like their ancestors, a stubborn and rebellious generation. —Psalm 78:8

One grandmother says she could both laugh and cry. Her adult children want her to eat organic local foods and bike instead of driving. They want to save the planet. But they don't notice what she learned about energy consumption while raising her family.

She insists that family values be passed along, but that they be stated in new language and styles. The environment is as important to her offspring as it is for her. And the young find it as difficult to live sacrificially as it was for her generation.

Verse 8 reflects this dilemma. While mourning "the stubborn and rebellious generation[s]" of the past, the writer hopes that the children will do better. By understanding how God acted in the past, they can live in God's ways now.

Young people do imitate the values of their parents—the values they really live by. They know when their elders derive joy, peace, and direction from God's leading. That gift can flow to children still unborn. —Mary Lou Cummings

For generation after generation, as our parent God, you have sustained us, taught us, and saved us from ourselves. Let me also trust you for the future.

* * * * * * * * * * * * * * *

Devotional 6

They ate and were well filled, for he gave them what they craved. —Psalm 78:29

I am a photo junkie. I take hundreds of pictures each year: Ethan's first summertime dive, Emma's first picnic, my husband's big catch, my parents' birthdays. I like to sit on the front porch with my albums and remember those times.

Verse 29 is a stroll down memory lane, picturing God, who faithfully responded to human need. When the Israelites were in the desert and they were hungry, God provided manna and quail from heaven. The people were assured that God could be trusted—that God accompanied and guarded them on their way.

Once in Canaan, the Promised Land, they read psalms to refresh their memories of the forty-year trek through the wilderness. They recalled that God loyally led and accompanied them, fulfilled their needs, and protected their interests. As they recalled God's actions, they knew—despite the hardships they endured in Egypt and in the desert—how blessed they were. *–Julie Ellison White*

Stroll down memory lane: picture the times and situations in which you felt God's accompaniment. May these snapshots give you strength for today.

* * * * * * * * * * * * * * *

Devotional 7

[God] chose his servant David, and took him from the sheepfolds . . . to be the shepherd of his people. . . . With upright heart he tended them. —Psalm 78:70, 72

I was born the last of five children, a so-called afterthought. My siblings are more than eight years older than I. Being late-born doesn't seem to wear off, even after fifty years. I'm still the kid brother. My loving siblings still like to tell me what to do.

David is also late-born. He is chosen over his older, seemingly more qualified brothers to lead Israel. By integrity and skill, David leads with a shepherd's heart.

But David has disadvantages. His brothers scorn him on the battlefield before his victory over Goliath (1 Samuel 17). But he demonstrates he can follow God through the choice and calling laid upon him.

We may have "disadvantages" due to our birth order, upbringing, or other circumstances. Yet we are called to follow God and apply our gifts to challenges we face. What are your calling and gifts? Go with your gifts, for God has chosen and will use you for divine purposes. *–David Wiebe*

O Lord, everything I have is a gift from you. Thank you. Please help me use what you've given me for your glory and calling.

Let praise continue

PSALM 104

* *

Opening

Psalm 104 praises the glory of God, who created the world in grandeur and order. The heavens, earth, water, moon, sun, and life on planet earth reflect how and why God did these in wisdom and grace. Sing hymns that celebrate the majesty of God in nature, such as "O Worship the King," "This Is My Father's World," and "I Sing the Mighty Power of God."

Understanding the Word

Psalm 104 is a beautiful hymn that mirrors the six days of creation. The writer does not tell us *about* God but offers statements of sustained praise to God. In early Christian worship, Psalm 104 was read on Pentecost. Verse 30 says, "When you send forth your spirit, they are created; and you renew the face of the ground." God's Spirit gives physical life to creation and spiritual life to God's created ones.

Psalm 104 is an ecology psalm. It praises God, who created and continues to create and renew the earth. It makes clear that God provided abundantly for all living things: water for animals (v. 10); nesting places for birds; grass for cattle (v. 14); mountains for wild goats (v. 18).

Not only are places set for humans and animals but so are times: at night the wild animals stir (v. 20), and as the sun rises, humans go to work (vv. 22-23). It is a picture of balance and harmony among God's creatures; humans must not despoil the environment—their habitat and ours.

* *

For the leader

Bring a hymn book.

1. Invite group members to close their eyes and imagine the most beautiful place on the earth they know. Invite them to share where and what they saw.

2. Invite four group members to read Psalm 104:1-4; 5-9; 10-13; 31-35.

Connecting with God's Word

Praise God as king of the heavens (104:1-4)

In the Ancient Near East, people believed the world came about when several gods were in conflict. But the Hebrew writer affirmed that the Lord, Yahweh, is the maker of the creation.

- This psalm can be seen as an expansion on the creation story in Genesis 1. Compare their similarities. Does this connection strengthen your faith in God's creative wonders and lead you to praise God?

- Thomas Aquinas said that "God is revealed in two volumes: Scripture and nature, but theology and the church have ignored creation." What is the church losing by ignoring creation? What does "creation-centered" spirituality teach us about God?

Praise God who created the earth (104:5-9)

In his book *Out of the Depths*, Bernhard Anderson says, "Israel inherited a picture of the universe that depicted the world as surrounded on every hand by 'the waters of chaos' which, at the time of creation, the Creator subdued and pushed back in order to give creatures space in which to live and perform their God-given tasks."[1] Unlike their pagan neighbors, Israel did not grant divine powers to waters. The waters serve God. From this perspective, the psalmist described the wonders of creation.

- Psalm 104 pictures a created order in which a benevolent God provides for all creatures. How do you reconcile this picture when nature seems out of control—when weather- and water-related disasters strike. How do you affirm God's control over the earth? How do you respond to those who view these events as signs of God's vindictiveness and anger?

- Does being in a natural environment make you think about God more than you would otherwise? Why or why not?

The sea (104:24-26)

The psalmist marvels that God created such a complex world and in wisdom made it just right. There are many creatures in the sea: huge whales, fearsome sharks, tiny seahorses, and hefty tuna. Added to the mix are ships made with human hands. Having this great, wide sea, God created Leviathan, the great sea beast, to play in the sea (v. 26). The Leviathan is one of the many sea creatures that inspires joy, not fear.

---

[1] Bernhard Anderson, *Out of the Depths* (Louisville, KY: Westminster John Knox Press, 2000), 111.

- How do you participate in caring for God's creation? How do you respect and care for such indispensable resources as clean water, clean air, and nonrenewable energy sources? Create a list of ways to protect the sea and share its bounty justly.

Life and death are in the hands of God (104:27-30)

God sustains all living things of the earth. Their very breath is dependent on God's grace. Creatures are aware of this (v. 27). When God hides the divine face from his creatures, "they are dismayed" (v. 29). Humans need to remember that their very lives depend on God. Verse 30 indicates God's continuous creation and renewal of the earth.

- God has given all living things a place and has provided for their needs. How does this psalm confirm or challenge your understandings of the relationship between humans and animals?

A praise song (104:31-35)

The psalmist exults in God, hoping God is pleased with the creation. The impulse to sing as a response to God is familiar to us. We use words and tunes to express how we feel.

Verse 35 calls for the disappearance of sinners. People are born with a propensity to sin. We sin because of our fear that we will not have what we need, because of personal failures, because of unrealistic expectations placed on us, and because of our lack of hope.

But sin is not the last word. We do not need to be in bondage. God can free us and other sinners too. Christ frees us from sin and empowers us to live in God's way.

- Compose a poem or hymn of praise exalting God for creation. Include reasons you enjoy and appreciate the wonders of God's creation.

- What part of nature interests you? Have you ever gathered autumn leaves, river-washed stones and pebbles, shells, feathers, or flowers? Have you ever drunk from a clear mountain stream? How conscious are you that God is a part of all this? Even Jesus says to consider the lilies of the field and the birds of the air (Matthew 6:25-30).

Closing

1. Name one way to treat God's creation with renewed respect and honor.

2. Sing a hymn of praise and thanks to God for the church, people, animals, and the life-supporting resources for the world to continue.

DEVOTIONALS

* * * * * * * * * * * * * * * * * * * *

Devotional 1

[You are] wrapped in light as with a garment. . . . You make the clouds your chariot, you ride on the wings of the wind.
—Psalm 104:2-3

Psalm 104 is pure poetic beauty. The vivid pictures of God's attire and God's actions were common in Ancient Near Eastern cultures, but they are fresh ways to think about the Creator. Pictures of God "wrapped in light," using the clouds as chariots, the wind as messenger, and fire and flame as ministers, stretch my appreciation of him. Who can ever exhaust his length and breadth, height and depth?

John Longhurst said, "The Lord is my snowplow driver. My path shall be clear." He came to this picture of God during a May snowstorm. In zero visibility, he had pulled off the road. When a snowplow appeared, he was able to follow it home.

Psalms encourage us to use our imaginations to understand God. Look for God in the ordinary. God is like my warm blanket on a cold night or a cold drink of water after a brisk walk. God is like the flashlight showing the way on a midnight walk or a loving shoulder to cry on in a time of trouble. *–Edna Dyck*

God, you are mysterious and wonderful. Help me to encounter you in new ways today.

* * * * * * * * * * * * * * *

Devotional 2

You cause the grass to grow for the cattle, and plants for people to use, to bring forth food from the earth. —Psalm 104:14

The psalmist poetically describes God's order in nature: the people and animals are fed with grass and other plants; night follows day, and each has its appointed function. Everything is under God's supervision. It is "good."

One morning I saw a blue heron in the creek. She stood motionlessly and then suddenly dipped into the water with her long beak, catching her lunch. Then she gracefully flew away. What a sight! Like the young lions in verse 21, she was seeking her "food from God."

Chief Seattle, a nineteenth-century chief of the Suquamish Indians, said in a speech in 1854, "We did not weave the web of life; we are merely a strand in it. Whatever we do to the web we do to ourselves, for all belongs to the Creator."

Spend some time outdoors, pondering God's creation. Observe creatures in the wild; think about how their lives are regulated. Watch the sun rise or set, the daylight come or go, and ponder God's goodness. Think about the marvelous rhythm in nature. *–Edna Dyck*

Creator God, we are in awe at your marvelous works! We are grateful that you are in charge.

* * * * * * * * * * * * * * *

Devotional 3

O Lord, how manifold are your works! In wisdom you have made them all; the earth is full of your creatures. —Psalm 104:24

One day, our daughter, Doreen, was walking our dog along the country road where we live. As they walked, Doreen observed that he likes to bark at and dash toward cows that stare through fences. We try to discourage that because farmers aren't happy to see their cows endlessly running. But that day, the cows kept coming back to the fence after our dog gave chase, as if they were in on the game and were enjoying teasing our dog.

This Scripture reminds us that the God who created the world loves the creatures and finds joy in them. Verse 26 refers playfully to "Leviathan that you formed to sport in [the sea]." Similarly, the cows were sporting with our dog. And Doreen enjoyed their play.

Let the animals you see today remind you of the enormous role they play in our lives, whether as food, companionship, sport, entertainment, or solace. God planned it. Let us rejoice in God's good works for this earth. –*Melodie Davis*

Lord, we thank and praise you for all your good creation and for the animals you have placed here.

* * * * * * * * * * * * * *
Devotional 4

When you send forth your spirit, they are created; and you renew the face of the ground. —Psalm 104:30

Pentecost celebrates the gift of the Holy Spirit. Psalm 104 is often read to remind us that God's Spirit is also at work in all creation. We are God's creation twice over. Our physical and spiritual lives are both the work of the Holy Spirit.

One time my wife and I were driving through the Rocky Mountains. We stopped and recited some of the great statements about God's creative grandeur in hymns and in the Bible. We were moved to awe, wonder, and worship.

At a Mennonite Church Canada assembly, we were moved to worship by the music, testimony, and preaching. We received a fresh "anointing for healing" as we considered the ways we have failed to see God's Spirit at work among the creatures and natural wonders of creation.

It was like receiving a fresh Pentecost–a universal reminder that "the whole creation has been groaning in labor pains until now" (Romans 8:22). All creation wants to be a voice of God's Holy Spirit to us. –*Bernie Wiebe*

Lord, teach us to listen and to hear the language of all creation as it speaks by your Holy Spirit.

* * * * * * * * * * * * * *
Devotional 5

When you send forth your spirit, they are created; and you renew the face of the ground. —Psalm 104:30

Before electricity came, our lives were regulated by sunrise and sunset. We completed our homework by the light of a kerosene lamp. We struggled to see the words and pictures. Shadows danced as the lamp's flame flickered on the walls.

When power came, as I began my homework, Mom turned on the switch. Light exploded into the room. Words and numbers were as clear as in the sunlight. No more shadows on the walls. A new way of living was now possible. Soon a refrigerator gave us ice-cold water and preserved our milk and leftovers.

In *The Divine Conspiracy: Rediscovering our Hidden Life in God*, Dallas Willard shares a similar experience. He notes that electricity changed lives when people took practical steps to rely on it.

Wonderful changes happen as we

"connect" to the Spirit, opening our minds and hearts to God's instruction, insight, comfort, and power. We become new creations: "the old has passed away; see, everything has become new" (2 Corinthians 5:17). –*Wally Sawatzky*

God, your Spirit lives with us and in us. May the Spirit renew and empower us for each situation we face today.

* * * * * * * * * * * * * * *
Devotional 6

I will sing to the LORD as long as I live; I will sing praise to my God while I have being. —Psalm 104:33

Psalm 104 ends as it began, in an exuberant call to praise. The psalmist, convinced that God will sustain the world and everything in it, promises lifelong devotion to the Creator.

But in these final verses, a shadow crosses this bright scene: sin brings this shocking thought: "Let sinners be consumed from the earth." The psalmist knows that some do not hold faith in God's creation and orderliness in the universe. For many, life is a disaster.

Following a terrorist bombing, one woman pleaded, "Help me find my son, my only son; he is the love of my life." She feared that he had been killed. Her prayer could have been, "Let sinners be consumed from the earth" (v. 35).

My world is orderly and right. I thank God for my beautiful world. I vow to praise God all my life, and I remember those in turmoil. May God grant me the courage to help bring God's order and song to those consumed by fear and chaos. –*Edna Dyck*

Lord, I praise you for the beautiful world you have created. Help me to keep my part beautiful and to praise you with my whole being.

* * * * * * * * * * * * * * *
Devotional 7

May my meditation be pleasing to him, for I rejoice in the LORD. —Psalm 104:34

When threatened, the bombardier beetle fires a substance from its tail. The temperature of its "stuff" is at the boiling point. After the attack, the beetle cleanses itself of the residue so it will not blow itself up. "O LORD, how manifold are your works!" (v. 24).

The psalmist calls us to meditate. He invites us to enjoy the created things: sun, moon, stars, fish, grass, and trees–even bombardier beetles. He wants us to know the well-being of a beautiful world. As we consider the wonders of nature, we encounter the glory of God.

Is meditation a lost art? Some of our greatest leaders were spiritually renewed through meditation, even amid dangerous upheavals. Jesus, before his ministry, was driven into the wilderness. Before Paul served as a church planter, he went to the silence of Arabia.

The practice of meditation is for all. Everyone can know the power of the secret place and the shut door. "May my meditation be pleasing to him" (v. 34). –*Marvin Hein*

Lord, help me to be quiet amid the world's hustle and bustle. Help me notice the awesome creation over which you rule. May my meditations be acceptable to you.

8

Don't be afraid

Psalm 121

* *

Opening

Psalm 121 reflects the experience of pilgrims who come to the temple in Jerusalem for the great festivals of God's people. It is also appropriate for their experience of returning home after such events. People today find assurance of God's care in their experiences as well. When have you heard the reading of this psalm? On what occasions was it read or repeated? How did it affect your life and that of your family or church community?

* *

For the leader

Bring a topographical map of the area surrounding Jerusalem.

1. Jerusalem is situated on a hill about 2,500 feet above sea level. It is surrounded by the Kidron and Hinnon and other lesser valleys. To enter the city, visitors must ascend several hills. Review the physical area around the city to discern the need for protection as pilgrims made their way up to the temple in the city.

- Have there been times when you traveled and were concerned about the safety of your route and your destination?

- Did you share with friends and family about your anxieties?

- Did you handle your stress through prayer or by reading or repeating this psalm? How helpful did you find these practices?

2. Numbers 6:24-26 has been linked to Psalm 121 as a benediction and prayer for travelers who are headed to their home after the festivals in Jerusalem. Some congregations receive this benediction at the close of worship. Perhaps some families repeat it when members go on a trip.

- Has this benediction been prayed on your behalf on important occasions?

- How were you strengthened by it?

3. Repeat this psalm as follows: Members of the study group chant verses 1-2 in the first person voice (I, my) then the leader chants verses 3-8 in the second person (you).

Understanding God's Word

Psalms 23 and 121 are among the best known in the Bible. Many people have memorized them and find comfort in their words. Both speak of the comfort and care God lavishes on humans who have the eyes to see and appreciate God's hand at work.

"Psalm 121 continues as one of the best known psalms in Christian liturgy, hymnody, and piety," states James H. Waltner, the author of *Psalms*. "The psalm has been used in services of baptism, comforting the bereaved, burying the dead, and in ministry to the addicted."[1]

Connecting with God's Word

Eyes lifted to the hills (121:1-4)

This psalm, along with about twelve others, is called a "song of ascent." It is thought that these psalms were recited during the pilgrimage festivals to Jerusalem and other Israelite worship sites. This psalm may also have been a closing benediction recited responsively. The pilgrim chants verses 1-2 in the first person voice (I, my) and the priest or leader chants verses 3-8 in the second person (you).

The pilgrims are reassured that God, who reigns over earth and heaven, is a ready helper. In the Ancient Near East, people thought of the mountains and hills as the dwelling places of the gods. Israel reflected that imagery in its own poetry about God. But Israel's belief went further. The affirmation of the second verse—"My help is from the LORD, maker of heaven and earth"— indicates that Yahweh, the God of Israel, is also the Creator. In the religions of Israel's neighbors, the creator god was distinct and distant from the gods that people prayed to for help in everyday life. Israel's God, however, is affirmed to be the same God who created heaven and earth.

- Psalm 121 is a favorite because it offers comfort and reassurance that God cares about us and is willing and able to meet our needs, whether spiritual, physical, psychological, or material. When do you turn to this psalm for help and comfort? Share times and experiences during which it has comforted you.

- Lifting our eyes to the hills does not change realities on the ground, but it does give us a different perspective. For example, in Genesis 21:14-19, Hagar and her son, Ishmael, run out of water in the wilderness. God opens Hagar's eyes and she sees a well of water. The well was there before, but she did not see it until God opened her eyes. Share experiences of

---

[1] James H. Waltner, *Psalms*, Believers Church Bible Commentary (Scottdale, Pa.: Herald Press, 2006), 593, 596.

times when you "lifted your eyes" and became aware of God's provision, help, and care.

- Verse 4 assures readers that God does not slumber and is always aware of people's needs. How does the awareness of this constant vigil on your behalf affect you? In what ways are you comforted by and confident in this knowledge? Describe how this feels.

The Lord as Protector (121:5-8)

In Greek mythology, the goddess Persephone returns to the underworld during the winter and arises each spring to usher in new growth. By contrast, Israel's God never rests or retreats. Yahweh, the psalmist says, is always watching over and caring for Israel.

Even today, the sun claims its victims through sunstroke or heat exhaustion during the long Middle Eastern summers. For most years, it does not rain at all in Israel for five months. People are very aware of the dangers of too much sun. The reference to the moon striking at night refers to an ancient belief that the moon has power to cause illness. Traces of this belief are found today among those who believe that the moon causes people to behave strangely.

The opening line of verse 7 reads, "The LORD will keep you from all evil," or "harm," as the *New International Version* and the *Tanakh* (the Jewish Publication Society translation) read. The word is also translated "bad." Protection is one of the things for which people rely on God.

- This psalm says that God will keep us from evil (bad, harm). Yet Christians do suffer in this life. How do you explain this in light of the assurance that God protects from evil? What does it mean to you to be kept from evil?

Closing

1. Describe one experience in which your life has been touched by Psalm 121.

2. Close by reading the psalm as you did in the beginning of the session. Treat it as a benediction for group members as they enter life in the week ahead.

DEVOTIONALS

* * * * * * * * * * * * * * * * * * * *
Devotional 1

I lift up my eyes to the hills—from where will my help come? My help comes from the LORD, who made heaven and earth.
—Psalm 121:1-2

As God's people walked toward Jerusalem, they sang Psalm 121. It included a confession of what the people believed about God and provided them with reassuring word pictures about the Lord's care.

The Lord gave them sure footing. He protected them around the clock. During the heat of the day and in the moonlit, shadow-filled night, the Lord's eyes never closed.

I made a bad decision based on deceptive advertising. During the sleepless nights and anxiety-filled days, I cried to the Lord for help. God walked with me during those bleak days. I felt the Lord's presence as I contacted those involved. I clung to the promise that God's Spirit would guide me. I believed that the Lord would answer my cries, that God would walk with me through my dark night.

Psalm 121 is not only a song for ancient pilgrims ascending to Jerusalem; it's equally appropriate for us today. God who watched over the people of Israel also watches over us today. *–Nancy Witmer*

Lord, I need your care and protection. Be my helper today and forever.

* * * * * * * * * * * * * * * * * * * *
Devotional 2

My help comes from the LORD, who made heaven and earth. —Psalm 121:2

The bigger hills and mountains are, the more they take our breath away. It's hard to pull our gaze away from their grandeur, even in our mind's eyes. In the days of this psalm, many people thought the high hills were sites where gods lived. They brought gifts to sacrifice to the gods of the "high places." They also adored the sun, the moon, and the stars.

But the poet of Psalm 121 quickly pulls back from "the hills," thinking only of God who helps us, who stays awake to care for us even when we are sleeping.

Some who lived among the Israelites worshipped the sun, moon, or stars, as well as the mountains. The Israelites knew that these were not gods. They knew that their God made them all. The lights in the heavens were made by their God, who controlled their motions and lights.

When tempted to look to "high places" for help, the psalmist reminds us that God is right at our side. *–Maynard Shelly*

God, the skies at night are vast and grand because you made them for us.

* * * * * * * * * * * * * *
Devotional 3

He who keeps you will not slumber. —Psalm 121:3

Did you notice how many times this psalm uses the word *keep*? I count five (vv. 3, 4, 5, 7, 8). The psalmist assures us that the one who watches over God's people does not doze off.

In verse 1, I imagine the psalmist gazing at the hills around Jerusalem that are peppered with idolatrous shrines. "I look up to the 'holy places' around me," he seems to say, "but can these gods help?" No, it is God alone who keeps vigil over his people by day and night.

During the Blitz of 1940, a woman was lying awake in her London home. As she tossed and turned, she heard God ask, "Why are you still awake?"

"I'm watching for bombers," she replied.

"Then you might as well go to sleep," God answered. "There's no point in both of us doing that."

Do you feel anxious? Alone? Perplexed? Remember, you are under the unblinking gaze of the God who loves you. —Helen Paynter

God-who-watches, I am glad to be the subject of your loving vigil, in my comings and goings, by day and by night.

* * * * * * * * * * * * * * *
Devotional 4

The LORD will keep you from all evil; he will keep your life. —Psalm 121:7

I like the King James Version rendering of this verse. Recent versions have lost this amazing wording: "[God] shall preserve thy soul."

We know that God doesn't always keep Christians or anyone else out of harm's way. Bad things happen to good people. My grandfather Ivan, at the young age of fifty-one, was killed instantly when he drove head-on into a tree on his way home from helping my mom and dad on their farm. I never knew him.

He might have had a heart attack or passed out. But why couldn't he have missed that tree? Did God keep him from

harm? No, but I have no doubt that God did preserve his soul.

My grandfather's Bible contains a footnote by the word *preserve*, directing readers to Psalm 97:10, which says, "[God] preserveth the souls of his saints." How much more comforting is this since we know that whatever happens, God is with us and will preserve our souls for all eternity. –*Melodie Davis*

God, thank you for your promise to keep us in your care, no matter what. We thank you for your providence, and we trust.

* * * * * * * * * * * * * * *
Devotional 5

The LORD will keep your going out and your coming in from this time on and forevermore. —Psalm 121:8

My wife and I moved cross-country. We had garage sales, changed our addresses, and packed boxes. In the turmoil, we made mistakes: missed a deadline, sold things we needed, and exchanged cross words. Sometimes we wanted to say, "Help!"

Psalm 121 was written for such times. When you move, when you sprain an ankle (v. 3), when you are overheated by the sun's heat (vv. 5-6), or when nocturnal lunacy threatens (v. 6), where do you find help? The psalmist looks first to the surrounding high places.

He reminds fellow travelers that there is no help on the Hills of Quick Fixes. Our help is the Lord. Five times the psalmist names the Lord "Yahweh." Six times he calls Yahweh our keeper.

Psalm 121 is for people who are moving—whether moving cross-country, driving in the fast lane, or walking with other pilgrims to our Jerusalem. But the psalm is not about us. It's about Yahweh, our keeper. The Lord watches over us. The Lord sees, knows, and watches. –*Lynn Jost*

O God, these are days when we can't keep an eye on everything. Thank you for the promise of your watchful keeping.

* * * * * * * * * * * * * *
Devotional 6

The LORD will keep your going out and your coming in from this time on and forevermore. —Psalm 121:8

A college student was hospitalized after she fell while rock climbing. As her nurse, I was at her bedside. For days she was strapped to a stryker frame, which had to be turned every two hours. On alternate turns, she faced the floor, then the ceiling.

Nightly her nightmares returned. She would wake up, screaming, crying, and straining against the straps. When she was facing down, I sat on the floor, patted her cheek gently, and cradled her face in my hands. "It's all right," I'd tell her. "You're not alone. I won't let you fall."

Many evenings we told her family, "You go home and sleep. We will take care of her."

God is with us in dark and lonely moments. When we are worried, we can rest because our Father never sleeps. When we wake in the night and call his name, he is there. Imagine hearing God say, "It's all right; I'm here and I will not let you fall." –*Gertrude M. Slabach*

Many nights, Lord, I worry. You said that you will watch over my coming and my going. Help me claim that promise so I can rest in you.

* * * * * * * * * * * * * *
Devotional 7

The LORD will keep your going out and your coming in from this time on and forevermore. —Psalm 121:8

Tommy is a front-door security guard for our apartment building. He greets each person with a cheery comment in Cantonese, Mandarin, or English.

Because he works both night and day, Tommy knows our schedules. "Much work for the teacher today," he says as I come home after dark. "You leave early for church?" he asks if we exit ahead of time on Sundays. "Mr. and Mrs. Driedger have party," he commented to Dave after his students came over for pizza. He asks about Dave's squash game if he sees his racquet. He helps me with the elevator door when I carry many grocery bags.

Tommy's knowledge of our "going out" and "coming in" makes us feel secure. Because we live far from our families, it is good that someone notes our presence and schedules.

The psalmist says that the Lord keeps track of us day and night. How blessed we are to have the services of such a great Security Guard! –MaryLou Driedger

What a comfort to know you are with me always, God. Grant me awareness of your guiding presence and greater trust in the security you provide.

Searched and known by God

PSALM 139

* *

Opening

1. Psalm 139 extols the all-knowing, ever-present, wonder-creating God.

   - How has this passage affected your life?

   - How have you experienced God's searching and knowing (vv. 1-6, 23-24)?

   - How comfortable are you that you have no escape from God's awareness?

   - How has the knowledge that God has fearfully and wonderfully created you affected your life decisions?

2. God's gifts make you a unique member of your church, community, and family. What gifts are you using with each group?

Understanding God's Word

Psalm 139 is hard to classify because it does not fit neatly into any of the three major psalm types. It is not a hymn of praise, or an informal song of thanksgiving, or a lament with a focus on complaint. Bernhard Anderson admits to tentatively listing Psalm 139 with the laments, as many scholars do, but he also sees in it elements of praise and wisdom.[1]

In his *Psalms*, Artur Weiser uses "omni" language to outline the first three sections of this psalm: God's omniscience (vv. 1-6), God's omnipresence (vv. 7-12), and God's omnificence (vv. 13-18). God, who is all-knowing, ever-present, and all-creating, is worthy of praise.[2]

While this psalm may not fit well into any one type, it clearly moves us to awe and praise. It leads us to transparency before God, to penitence, and to a desire for openness in God's presence.

---

[1] Bernhard Anderson, *Out of the Depths* (Louisville, KY: Westminster John Knox Press, 2000), 91.
[2] Artur Weiser, *Psalms* (Louisville, KY: Westminster John Knox Press, 1962), 802–805.

For the leader

Bring a gift inventory or assessment tool used by your congregation or area conference.

Read Psalm 139:1-18, 23-24 antiphonally. As a guide, use number 823 in *Hymnal: A Worship Book*.[3] Invite the men to read the light part and the women the dark part. Or you read the light part and the study group reads the dark part. Invite one member to close by reading verses 23-24.

Connecting to God's Word

O Lord, you know me (139:1-6)

The psalmist is struck with the thought of being known "inside out" by God—felt, searched, inspected, or "read like a book." Today we might think of an exhausting interview or a personality inventory taken under a trained counselor. Did the ancient poet think of God as a master psychoanalyst who could figure out clients better than the clients themselves? Or was God the master crystal-ball gazer who could see ahead and predict the future?

Verse 5 speaks of being hemmed in, perhaps as a complaint. But we could turn this around and read it as a comfort: God knows all we have been through and what is ahead and, therefore, as a loving and compassionate God, will know how to care for us.

The double use of *know* in verses 1-2 connects with knowledge "too wonderful for me" in verse 6, a positive attitude of awe, of reverence, rather than a negative cramping or hemming in. Isaiah 55:8—"For my thoughts are not your thoughts, nor are your ways my ways"—comes to mind.

- How do you feel about a God who knows so much more than we are even aware?

Where can I flee from your presence? (139:7-12)

This part focuses on the ever-present One. The farthest point up ("the heavens") and the farthest point down ("Sheol") are all within God's sphere. For the psalmist, the farthest point east ("take the wings of the morning") and the farthest point west ("the sea") are within God's creation. If your hide-and-go-seek rules restrict you to hiding in the house, you will be found. If this poet can hide only within God's universe, he too will be found.

- Do you find God's guiding hand and his right hand that holds (v. 10) threatening or reassuring and sustaining?

- How do you respond to a God who formed you, knows you, sees you, and accompanies you? In what ways do you identify with the psalmist's response?

---

[3] *Hymnal: A Worship Book* (Scottdale, Pa.: Mennonite Publishing House, 1992).

- The darkness is no problem for God. How is God's comforting presence like your guard dog that protects your home or keeps you safe as you go on walks?

You knit me together in my mother's womb (139:13-18)

"Knit" and "woven" (vv. 13, 15) are needlework and fabric terms to help us marvel at God's involvement in our formation. The ancients believed that life began before birth. The intricacy of the embryo and the delicacy of the before-birth process move the psalmist to exclaim, "I praise you . . . your works are wonderful" (v. 14).

Verses 16-17 move beyond marveling at God's involvement in formation to suggest God's foreknowledge and predetermination ("In your book were written all the days that were formed for me," v. 16). God had thoughts about and plans for you, even before your birth. You are God's custom-designed you.

- This psalm underscores that you were not an accident. When you deprecate yourself unduly, you are putting down God's work. Who has encouraged you to respect and praise God for who you are and the unique contributions you make to your family and church?

- Our bodies are to be cared for and not abused. How have you applied this?

- This psalm gives a unique perspective about humans. We are the "crown of creation" and are known as individuals. Are you comfortable with this?

Search me and know my heart (139:23-24)

Verses 23-24 are the crowning response to God's thorough familiarity, steady presence, ever-seeing eyes, and preplanning. The psalmist willingly opens himself to God as if to say, "Oh God, I want you to know me, to see me, to stay with me, and to continue the development you started in me before my birth. Is there anything offensive in me?" the implication being, ". . . so I can change my ways." The psalmist may have been saying, "I am not intentionally sinning, doing anything wicked, but if I am even doing something that annoys you, please let me know." What transparency! What a desire to please!

- In what circumstances has God revealed his unconditional love to you and directed your obedience to go another way?

- Verses 23-24 are the crowning response of the psalmist to God. What words would you use to express your thoughts to God?

Closing

1. Express thanks for one gift God has given you that you use often.

2. Close by reading Psalm 139 as outlined on page 57.

Psalm 139

Devotionals

* *

Devotional 1

O Lord, you have searched me and known me. —Psalm 139:1

Lillian was a wise woman. She was a musician, teacher, and pastoral caregiver. Her sensitivity related to the burdens she carried. As a child, she had suffered because of her family's image. As an adult, her public gifts were often questioned.

As a church leader, she protected all confidences. When I complained about injustices experienced by leaders, she would smile and say, "God knows!" The phrase described her relationship with God.

The psalmist glories in what God knows. Verse 1 and 4 each say, "O Lord, you know." Stanza 1 ends in verse 6 by expressing wonder at God's intimate acquaintance of him: "Such knowledge is too wonderful for me."

While we may find God's awareness invasive, the psalmist finds it comforting. When trouble comes, God knows! When my paths are delightful, God knows. God's knowledge goes beyond information. In our daily struggles, God knows all that we face.
–*Lynn Jost*

Lord, I am overwhelmed by your far-reaching knowledge of my life. You know everything about me. Help me to relax in your knowledge today.

Devotional 2

You know when I sit down and when I rise up. —Psalm 139:2

I accompanied my wife to an event sponsored by a group with which she is connected. She introduced herself to another attendee, who greeted me using my first name. I thought, "Who are you?" and "What do you know about me?"

You may have met a stranger who knows you, or something about you, perhaps because of the name of your spouse, your parents, or one of your siblings. It feels good to know that someone is interested enough to check our listing in the phone book or in the church directory. We feel flattered when we are recognized and known.

But when does personal knowledge become uncomfortable? Someone knowing the make and model of my car would not frighten me if I knew he was a car buff. But if he knew my personal information, I would raise my guard. In John 4:29, the woman at the well said of Jesus, he "told me everything I have ever done." But being known so deeply by Jesus was positive for her.
–James R. Engle

God, I am grateful that you know all about me and will guide me when I am resting and when I am active.

* * * * * * * * * * * * * *
Devotional 3

O Lord, you have searched me and known me. You know when I sit down and when I rise up. —Psalm 139:1-2

When I was a child living in India, our family would sometimes retreat from the heat of our home to the cool refreshment of the hills. Nearby was a church with a massive bell tower. On its facade was painted a great eye.

I was told that it was the all-seeing eye of heaven. It appeared to gaze at one constantly. I found it unsettling to think that it was following me during my holidays. At night, it seemed to gaze through the darkness. In the morning, I would creep up behind a grove of bamboo to find that it was still watching me.

Years later, I sat in a concert hall, listening to Ethel Waters. Her signature piece included the line "His eye is on the sparrow, and I know he watches me." She sang it with the abandon of a grateful love. She sang as one who finds beneath that eye a sweet harbor of release, warmth, and safety. God, let me live beneath the gaze of such an eye! *–Jonathan Larson*

That burning eye aflame with love has come to rest on me, and traces its radiant wake upon a darkened sea.

* * * * * * * * * * * * * *
Devotional 4

Such knowledge is too wonderful for me. —Psalm 139:6

When my wife, Jeanne, says something about me, I think, *She knows me better than I thought.* I find comfort in this: even though she knows my faults, she stays with me.

At the same time, she doesn't know everything about me. While we carry secret thoughts that our loved ones don't know, God does. God "is acquainted with all [our] ways" (v. 3) but does not leave us.

When two people fall in love, they want to learn all they can about each other, their history, their family, their hobbies, their dreams. As their knowledge grows, so does their intimacy. At times they may learn things that test their relationship. Will she still love me if she knows this? Will he still love me if he knows my hopes? When Jeanne learned some of my secrets and still loved me, I felt stronger as a person and my desire to love her deepened.

We cannot comprehend God's knowledge of us. It's "too wonderful" (v. 6), too full of awe and wonder. Being known and still being loved is awesome. It motivates us to love God back. *–Gordon Houser*

I'm so grateful, Lord, that you know everything about me yet still love me.

* * * * * * * * * * * * * *
Devotional 5

Where can I go from your spirit? —Psalm 139:7

As I walked home from elementary school, I threw snowballs at cars and houses. When I hit the window of one house, a woman yelled at me. I ran home and hid in my room.

Throwing snowballs may not seem evil, but I wanted to hide. I thought I would not be discovered if I stayed out of sight. Soon the phone rang, my mother found me, and we walked to the woman's house, where I apologized.

Psalm 139 is clear: there is no hiding place from God. This may be scary to those who want to hide their actions. But in the end, it's comforting. While it was hard to face that woman and admit my wrong, I felt better afterward.

In worship, we pray that God be present. But God is always present. The prayer is for our benefit. While we cannot hide from God, who sees all actions, we can be thankful for his always-present mercy. *–Gordon Houser*

Thank you, God, that you see everything I do. Teach me the comfort of your constant presence. Help me to live in your light.

* * * * * * * * * * * * * * *

Devotional 6

*I am fearfully and wonderfully made.
—Psalm 139:14*

Eighty percent of women are not satisfied with their appearance. Men are anxious about their ability to be productive. When we look in the mirror, do we lament our weight, our thinning hairline, or our lack of muscle? Or do we thank God for the way we are?

In college, I responded to another's query, "How are you?" by saying, "I am fearfully and wonderfully made." I wanted to remind myself of this truth. The biblical mirror reflects us truthfully. It conveys a radical, countercultural message: we are fearfully and wonderfully made–God formed us in the womb.

I have a long-term disability. I wish I could do all that I want to do. I struggle to believe that God can use me as I am. The psalmist assures us that despite our limitations, we are a wonder, created by God. My health disability reminds me of my dependence on God and others. How "vast" are God's thoughts (v. 17)! *–Gordon Houser*

We praise you, O God, that we are fearfully and wonderfully made.

* * * * * * * * * * * * * * *

Devotional 7

I praise you, for I am fearfully and wonderfully made. Wonderful are your works; that I know very well. —Psalm 139:14

During a visit to their ruins, I learned much about the Puebloans. They were sophisticated astronomers and persistent farmers. Their pictographs and petroglyphs are compelling. While they made goals that would take centuries to accomplish, they provided for their basic daily needs.

The Puebloans were shorter than people today. They lived only thirty-five to forty years and had a high infant mortality rate. Since they ground corn on stone pads with stone pestles, fine sand mixed with their flour ground down their teeth and exposed the nerves. The people suffered from tremendous dental anguish. Yet their work endures.

All God's many peoples and nations are beautiful. They are priceless treasures, not commodities to be exploited, remade, or ignored. Learning about the nations that share our planet, both now and those who lived centuries ago, makes one thing perfectly clear: they, like us, are fearfully and wonderfully made. *–Frank Ramirez*

Search me, O God, and know my heart; test me and know my thoughts. See if there is any wicked way in me, and lead me in the way everlasting (Psalm 139:23-24).

Worthy of praise

Psalm 145

* *

Opening

1. Psalm 145 is a song of praise. Sing a hymn of praise, such as "I owe the Lord a morning song," "Sing praise to God who reigns," "Praise, I will praise you, Lord," and "Great is the Lord." The hymn "We would extol thee" is based on Psalm 145.

2. Invite group members to share some of their highest moments of worship. Psalm 145 encourages believers to praise God in their own ways and to share their praise tradition with the young. In what ways do you praise? In what ways does your congregation encourage the young to praise God?

3. Read Psalm 145 responsively as follows:

   Leader: vv. 1-2 (introduction)

   Group: v. 3 (acknowledges that the transcendent God is "unsearchable")

   Leader: vv. 4-7 (activities of our transcendent Lord)

   Group: vv. 8-9 (recitation of the creed from Exodus 34:6-7)

   Leader: vv. 10-13 (themes from the creed and introduction to theme of God's kingdom)

   Group: vv. 14-20 (description of the nature of God's kingship)

   All: v. 21 (leader and group together repeat the call to praise God)

* *

For the leader

Bring paper and pencils for group members to write statements of praise to God.

Understanding God's Word

Psalm 145 is centered on God as worthy of praise. While there are a few references to God's creative activity, greatness and awesome works (vv. 10, 15-16), most refer to the history, people, and kingdoms. Psalm 145 is a hymn of praise to God, who is the Creator.

Psalm 145 uses numerous terms for praise. The people praising vary from "I" to "they." The emphasis shifts to the object of the praise (vv. 8-9), to speak to the Lord as "you" or "your," and sometimes to speak about the Lord as "he" or "his."

Connecting with God's Word

I will exalt you (145:1-3, 21)

Psalm 145 begins by expressing the poet's intention to praise God. In the first two verses, we see the word praise plus two synonyms, *bless* and *extol*. The extent of praise includes "every day" and "forever and ever," pointing to a frequent and enduring attitude of praise. The One being praised, God, is addressed as king, before the psalmist tells of God's mighty acts and wonderful works (vv. 4-7). These include kingly historical activities, as well as activities in nature and prehistory. Verse 21 returns to the theme of verse 1 and repeats the same ideas. Not only the psalmist but "all creatures" will bless his name.

- Make a list or call out the various words for praise used in this psalm.

They will speak, tell, and celebrate (145:4-7, 10-12)

Praise and celebration move beyond the individual to the group. "They" in verses 4-7 refers to "one generation . . . to another" in verse 4. "They" in verse 11 goes back to all God has made (vv. 9-10) or the "faithful" (v.10).

Now the spotlight shifts from the individual to "all." The culmination— the Z (Hebrew *tav*) of praise—is for "all flesh" to praise the name of the Lord, which returns to and repeats the A (Hebrew *aleph*) opening praise of verse 1, now expanded from "I" to "all flesh."

The different expressions for "praise" continue to pile up, ranging from "meditate" to "speak" to "sing." What the praising ones "tell" is abstract: "works," "mighty acts," "glorious splendor of majesty," "wonderful works," "awesome deeds," and "greatness." Whether the "works" are meant primarily as cosmic creative acts, works on behalf of all creatures, or historical acts on behalf of people(s), all of these and more are attributed to the Lord, and the Lord is worthy of praise.

- Which words reflect your personal preferences for praise? What terms require or assume a group or congregation? What terms work better for an inward personal or private response?

- How does your congregation encourage believers to praise God in their own ways and by sharing their practices of praise with future generations?

The Lord is gracious (145:8-9)

We may be surprised to find verse 8, a spectacular verse, tucked away within an acrostic that consists of rather flat repetition. But here it is—and it is worthy of special attention. This golden nugget celebrates the grace, compassion, patience, and steadfast love of the Lord.

For those who have not yet noticed the Lord's grace and compassion in the Old Testament, this verse is a good place to start. Verse 8 echoes Exodus 34:6, in which Moses sees God's self-revelation from the back and between the clefts of the rock at Mount Sinai at a time and place of high drama and of great revelation and insight.

Verse 9 is somewhat anticlimactic. It pales beside the richness of verse 8. But it does remind us that these great qualities of the Lord do not just remain shut up within God's keeping; they benefit "all that he has made." God's gracious qualities extend to humans, likely to all creatures, and perhaps to all created things.

- Look up other biblical passages where variations of this statement are made (Numbers 14:18; Nehemiah 9:17-18; Psalm 86:15, 103:8; Jonah 4:2).

- Why should God be praised? Verses 8 and 9 answer that question. It is not God's power or might that are mentioned first, but it is God's grace, compassion, and love. What does this say to you about the primary nature of God?

God the king (145:10-20)

God is the ideal king. As king, God sustains the weak and the needy; those who call on him are answered; and those who cry to him are saved. God brings justice to the oppressed and punishment to the oppressors.

- Are these the attributes you would expect of a king? Do they remind you of the kingdom of God as fulfilled in Jesus? How have you experienced God's kingly actions?

Closing

1. Ask the following questions, allowing a minute or two of quiet for each one: What are your reasons for praising God? In what ways has God been gracious and compassionate to you? When has God been slow to anger and rich in love toward you? Write short statements of praise to God for an activity from their past or for one that is happening now.

2. Close by reading Psalm 145 responsively as outlined in the beginning. Or invite group members to share their praise statements.

DEVOTIONALS

Devotional 1

Every day I will bless you, and praise your name forever and ever. —Psalm 145:2

My daily routine is to stop at the same place for coffee on my way to work. At work, I park in the same spot and check my email before I begin anything. And I pick up the kids at the same time.

I regret that sometimes I haven't taken time to pray, reflect on Scripture, or listen to God speaking through the events of the day.

Psalm 145 reminds us that praising God is one activity that must happen every day. We must tell God how great and worthy of praise he is. We must celebrate his abundant goodness to us.

One way to make praise part of my daily routine is to see God in everything I do. Now I praise God for my children. I thank God for my work and ministry. I celebrate the abundance of food in my cupboards and on grocery store shelves. I see God in my whole life and praise God every day. *–Jayne Byler*

Today, God, when I am caught up in my daily routines, remind me of your presence. May I give you the praise you deserve.

Devotional 2

Great is the Lord, and greatly to be praised; his greatness is unsearchable. —Psalm 145:3

Heinrich Duerksen and family fled to the Crimea after the Russian Revolution. By 1929, life in Russia was intolerable, so the Duerksens and many others went to Moscow to request exit papers to Germany. More than five thousand immigrants arrived in Germany and were offered asylum in the Chaco wilderness of Paraguay.

The early years were very hard. The crops didn't grow, food was scarce, and many died. In 1947 Heinrich was selected administrator of the Fernheim colony, and he served twenty-one years.

I met Heinrich in Paraguay in May 2001. He told stories about those early years. "It was so hard," he said repeatedly with tears. "But we survived. You know, it was all grace–God's grace." As I rose to leave, in a faltering voice, Heinrich said, "I know that my Redeemer lives." Tears blurred my eyes. I had seen greatness and had been touched by grace.

Heinrich died three months later. I will not forget his unfaltering faith. Grace and faith live on in those he knew. *–Anne Neufeld Rupp*

Thank you for the wonderful gifts you give even in times when everything seems to be going wrong. Help us to see your hand touching our lives.

Devotional 3

The Lord is gracious and merciful, slow to anger and abounding in steadfast love. —Psalm 145:8

Psalm 145, an acrostic psalm, uses the ABCs to praise God. It is a bridge psalm, concluding with a series of laments and moving toward the doxology of hallelujahs in verses 146-150.

The heart of the psalm is Israel's confession of faith (vv. 8-9). First declared by the Lord in Exodus 34:6-7, these phrases appear five more times in the Hebrew Bible. In Hebrew, the key words *merciful* and *compassion* come from a root word for *womb*. God's care is motherly; he hears the cries of children at night.

The Lord is "slow to anger." Literally, the Lord has a long nose—a Hebrew idiom describing a person who doesn't have a short fuse. While God punishes (Exodus 34:7), his inclination is to extend mercy. The Lord abounds in steadfast love—that is a covenant love of deep commitment, not obligation.

This psalm calls us to meditate on God's goodness. Ponder who God is and what God does. Make known the name of our God to all. –Lynn Jost

Lord, you nurture us like a mother. I praise you that you are loving, just, and protective.

* * * * * * * * * * * * * *

Devotional 4

The LORD is good to all, and his compassion is over all that he has made. —Psalm 145:9

Lebanon is a small country with majestic mountains, expansive Mediterranean beaches, and lofty cedars. Tourists flock to this "Switzerland of the Middle East." In thinking of "all that God has made," Lebanon's splendor impressed us resident aliens.

Unfortunately, Lebanon's beauty is marred by careless human activity. Beirut is often covered with dense, sickening smog from too many vehicles. Greedy developers scalp sand from the beaches and ravage hillsides with illegal quarries. The shores are polluted with sewage, trash, and oil. "Lord, have compassion on your creation!"

In facing these issues, Lebanon is not alone; environmental problems are global. Believers who ponder this psalm think about God's glorious handiwork and hope that humans will not ruin the earth.

Believing that God is concerned for creation can result in gratitude as well as care for the way we treat this planet. So we ask, "Does our gratitude for the beauty and marvels of God's creation include our resolve to care for God's handiwork?" –Ken Seitz

Cause us today, Creator, to join you in cherishing all you have made, including fellow humans. May our actions consistently show gratitude and model your compassion.

* * * * * * * * * * * * * *

Devotional 5

All your works shall give thanks to you, O LORD, and all your faithful shall bless you. —Psalm 145:10

Edward Wilson, a Harvard biology professor who won two Pulitzer Prizes, lost the sight in one eye as a child. In adolescence, he lost part of his hearing. He struggled with math and suffered from dyslexia. Yet his discovery of hundreds of new species gave us insights into God's greatness. We thank God for them.

In the bays of Antarctica, the coldest marine habitats on earth, water is cold enough to turn normal blood into ice. Yet fish live and thrive there, thanks to an antifreeze element generated within their own bodies.

In the boiling water of springs at the bottom of the sea, scientists discovered one-celled microorganisms that thrive in waters up to 230 degrees Fahrenheit (110 Celsius).

In the heat of deserts, a collection of plants, insects, and reptiles adapt to survive. And in the perpetual darkness of the world's deepest and dampest caves live numerous insects that feed on fungi and bacteria. There is nowhere on earth where God's greatness will not be seen. –Doug Snyder

We give you thanks, our God, for your marvelous creation and work.

Devotional 6

You open your hand, satisfying the desire of every living thing. —Psalm 145:16

A small child holds tightly to her mother's hand as they cross the street—the hand of trust. A young man extends his hand to the young woman walking by his side—the hand of love. A hiker reaches out to help his friend to the top of the steep incline—the hand of assistance.

God's open hand extends to us in many ways. God is faithful like a lover (v. 13-14) and nearby like a friend or a parent (v. 18).

God meets our needs unconditionally—loving us, welcoming us, helping us, and seeking our trust. God gives us food "in due season" with an open hand, "satisfying the desire of every living thing."

At Thanksgiving, we acknowledge God's hand for material gifts. But every day we must recognize that our Maker supplies us with all we need, including the unseen gifts of love, affirmation, and a sense of belonging. *—Amy Dueckman*

As my mouth speaks the praise of the Lord, blessing your holy name forever, may my hand be extended to your open one.

Devotional 7

The Lord is near to all who call on him, to all who call on him in truth. —Psalm 145:18

My mother's friend found life difficult after her husband's death. She said, "When I think I cannot go on, something happens. God helps me, and I can go on."

Many gospel songs affirm God's constant presence. "I need thy presence every passing hour," says one. "What but thy grace can foil the tempter's power?" says another.

Lina Zook Ressler, a missionary in India in the early 1900s, became desperately ill. The local doctors thought she was pregnant, but a British doctor discovered and removed a large ovarian cyst. During this crisis, Esther Ebersole Lapp stayed with Lina and nursed her back to health. Years later Lina recalled how Esther sang, "Be not dismayed whate'er betide. God will take care of you." Lina believed that song brought her back to life.

We can be reminded of God's constant presence by singing or hearing gospel songs, by recalling words of Scripture, by observing nature, and by calling on God whenever we are in need. *—Elaine Sommers Rich*

Thank you, Lord, that you are always near as I call on you often for help and strength.

CPSIA information can be obtained at www.ICGtesting.com
Printed in the USA
BVOW032354041012

302065BV00006B/8/P